Wall Street, Trade, and the New Economy

Volume III

The New Economy

For information about permission to reproduce selections from this book, write to
SWIFT Act Alliance, 1900 W Chandler Blvd, STE 15-285, Chandler, AZ 85224.
Email: info@swiftact.com

Cover design by Shon Quannie
Website: www.4x-media.com

ISBN: 978-1530561841

Library of Congress Control Number: 2016904560
CreateSpace Independent Publishing Platform, North Charleston, SC

Volume III - Contents

Figures and Illustrations

The Tyranny of Wall Street

As shown in Volume 2, the decline of American industry financed the rise in stock values, as corporate restructuring was used to create high prices for company shares.

The focus on stock values also provided the context for offshoring, as manufacturing was moved to low wage countries to raise profits.

The financial revolution in American business was also aided by Wall Street influence in the Treasury Department.

For example, offshoring accelerated dramatically after 1997, when foreign currencies throughout Asia were devalued.

Those devaluations were orchestrated by officials in the U.S. Treasury, as part of an overall plan to pay off international loans to Western banks.

The impact was to make imports cheaper, and create even more incentive for offshoring by U.S. multinationals.

This is only one of many examples of Wall Street influence, in which official policy has come to represent financial interests, at the expense of American industry.

Promotion of finance has also been fully bipartisan over a long period.

Bipartisan support enabled the Wall Street takeover of American business that led to offshoring by U.S. multinational companies.

Bipartisan consensus established Wall Street dominance of the economy that has run American industry out of business.

There is no greater threat to our society and to free enterprise than this bipartisan consensus.

Wall Street owes no allegiance to our values, to our national interest, or even to the basic principles of democracy.

But government represents Wall Street because politicians have been captured by money in politics.

That reality, in a word, is tyranny.

But the tyranny of Wall Street is not inevitable.

After all, it was resistance to the tyranny of taxation without representation that led to American independence.

We can take a stand and fight for our national interest and our hard won liberty.

Today that means taking on Wall Street, by joining together in a bipartisan alliance to confront it.

Organization

In 2011 the Occupy Wall Street movement was joined by tens of thousands of protesters in this country, and then by hundreds of thousands throughout Europe and around the world.

While Occupy was politically left of center, it was non-partisan in its criticism of Wall Street ties to the Obama administration and the Democratic Party.

The movement reflected opposition to Wall Street and unrestricted trade -- sentiment that isn't represented in either political party.

I was struck by similarities with the anti-NAFTA campaign of Ross Perot, who won nearly 20 million votes in the 1992 election.

In the aftermath of the 2008 financial crisis, the economy fell into the worst recession since the Great Depression of the 1930s.

All too often, the cause of the Great Recession is explained in financial terms, like the role played by derivatives in collapse of the housing market.

In reality that financial complexity was only the tip of the iceberg.

While for most of us the financial story sounds like Greek, the more important story behind it is seldom told.

My writing this book is an effort to tell that story in a way that gives you a handle on what has happened to the economy.

Organization is shown for all six sections in the series. This volume covers sections four, five, and six.

I: Fundamentals

Section 1 explains the dynamics of two models that show how economies grow, and how they stagnate.

These simple models can be used to compare different aspects of the economy at different points in time, and are referred to throughout the series.

Section 1 also provides an overview of today's New Economy and explains how it differs from the model of growth and why it doesn't work.

II: Background

Section 2 covers historical background that illustrates the fundamental principles outlined in the models of growth and stagnation.

Economic fundamentals in the period leading to the Great Depression of the 1930s were the same as those that led to the 2008 financial crisis.

Understanding those underlying similarities is essential to preventing a repeat of the Great Depression.

Policies implemented in this country in the 1930s, and adopted in Europe and Japan after World War II, brought long term growth accompanied by financial stability, low unemployment, and low inflation.

We need a clear understanding of what happened to disrupt that growth, and what it would take today to have it re-established.

Stagnation in the 1970s was defined by high levels of unemployment that coincided with high inflation in the same period.

From the mid-1960s through the early 1970s, presidents Johnson and Nixon pursued expansive economic policy that proved inflationary.

There were also crop failures in 1970 that drove up the price of commodities before the rise in oil prices.

Then in 1973 the price of oil tripled, which dramatically raised the cost of goods produced in manufacturing.

In 1974, price controls that had been imposed by President Nixon were lifted, so that pent up demand was also a factor contributing to inflation.

Thereafter, the price of oil doubled again between April 1979 and April 1980.

While these developments provided the context for inflation, by the late 1970s the focus had shifted to the idea that growth in wages was the root cause of inflation.

That juncture was the origin of policy that created the New Economy, which was and has remained fully bipartisan.

III: The Impact of Ideas
Section 3 outlines the impact of *anti-inflation policy* that emerged in the late 1970s, and continued through the late 1990s.

Once full employment came to be seen as inflationary, official policy came to embrace slower rates of growth that were considered non-inflationary.

Slow growth and artificially high levels of unemployment have had serious long term consequences for the economy.

While overall growth has been slower, the composition of that growth has changed to reflect the growth of finance instead of production, and job growth in services instead of manufacturing.

Section 3 also explains the shift from *anti-inflation policy* to support for asset bubbles in the stock and housing markets.

This *asset inflation policy* drove the housing bubble, intentionally created by Federal Reserve chair Alan Greenspan, which collapsed in the 2008 financial crisis.

IV: Globalism and Decline
Section 4 explains the way the U.S. economy operates within the world economy.

The way the balance of payments system works

- U.S. trade deficits are matched by inflows of foreign capital, and
- those inflows of foreign capital are used to finance deficits in the federal budget

But the way the balance of payments system works isn't a partisan issue.

When there's no conflict between the political parties, the media treats the issue as though it isn't news worthy.

This leads to under-reporting, leaving the public unaware of a critical flaw in how the New Economy operates.

Along the same lines, globalization of production through supply chains has fundamentally changed the meaning of trade.

Trade in finished products between countries has been replaced, *by trade in components* among production centers around the world.

The result is that both the value added in production and the jobs created by manufacturing have been moved out of the country.

Reporting on the issue is muted, because there's no conflict between the political parties when it comes to trade.

This bipartisan consensus on unrestricted trade has left the U.S. economy stripped of productive capacity and unable to create jobs.

V: The Wall Street/Trade Complex
Section 5 traces the rise of global finance that occurred in tandem with the globalization of production.

In the 1990s an excess of international lending drove booms in Mexico and throughout Asia that ultimately collapsed.

The response from the U.S. Treasury department was to orchestrate bailouts of Western banks through international loan agreements.

Those bailouts were based on loan guarantees and currency devaluation for the countries involved.

The result was acceleration of offshoring and unprecedented growth of the U.S. trade deficit, driven by imports from low wage countries.

Wall Street influence in the Treasury Department has done lasting damage to the U.S. economy, in both Democratic and Republican administrations.

Section 5 also provides a case study on China's strategic trade policy, which includes a range of incentives for U.S. multinationals to offshore production.

The case study on China also includes discussion of child labor and the number of children with industrial occupations throughout Asia.

VI: End Game

Section 6 evaluates the impact of the New Economy and the consequences of continuing political support that serves to perpetuate its contradictions.

Between 1998 and 2010 the U.S. trade deficit with low wage countries brought the loss of more than 23 million jobs.

The response to this unprecedented job loss was bipartisan rhetoric about reliance in the New Economy on services instead of manufacturing.

The reality is that service sector jobs are even more susceptible to offshoring than are jobs in manufacturing.

Princeton economist Alan Blinder, a former vice chairman of the Federal Reserve, estimates between 30 million and 40 million jobs in this country are susceptible to offshoring.

Meanwhile leading figures in both political parties speak of a New Economy, based on innovation and new jobs in the service sector.

The reality is that offshoring drives the destruction of American industry and disintegration of the U.S. economy.

Section 6 concludes with discussion of the bailout function of the federal government.

The risk of financial collapse poses an even greater threat to the economy today than in 2008.

The largest banks are now much larger, while unregulated trading in derivatives is backed by federal deposit insurance.

When the next Wall Street crisis requires government bailout, the losses involved will bankrupt the Treasury.

Conclusion: Mandate for Reform

Bipartisan consensus continues to support unregulated finance and unrestricted trade with low wage countries.

The consequences have been devastating.

Financial speculation has become far more profitable than productive investment, both domestically and all over the world.

At the same time, the pattern of world development creates too little demand to support markets for American goods.

The result has been distorted development of the world economy.

The U.S. economy has been both a driver and a victim of this development, and is now at risk of irreversible decline.

SWIFT Act is a collection of proposals to restructure the economy and reverse the damage done by Wall Street influence through money in politics.

The New Economy

Globalism and Decline

Prior to the 1980s, trade deficits were considered detrimental to the economy.

Trade deficits bring demand leakage, because every dollar spent on imports is a dollar not spent on domestic products.

This view of trade deficits changed with the discovery that trade deficits are matched by corresponding inflows of foreign capital.

Those inflows of foreign capital allowed Reagan to finance deficit spending without the consequences of inflation.

U.S. trade deficits have served as the driver of export led growth in the developing world.

The corresponding development has been the deindustrialization of America, as production has been offshored to low wage countries.

Offshoring has transformed the meaning of trade.

Component production in multiple countries is now integrated through global networks, serving to undermine national production.

This brings the loss of large scale employment that otherwise would have been generated through supply chains, and through the impact of re-spending in the national economy.

The impact has been to sever the link between local production centers and the national economies in which they were previously integrated.

American foreign policy has also promoted deregulation of foreign capital in poor countries.

Financial deregulation has exacerbated boom and bust cycles that lead ultimately to devaluation of poor country currencies.

Devaluation allowed poor countries to repay loans by building up trade surpluses with the U.S., causing an explosion of our trade deficit.

This high dollar policy serves financial interests, as well as the interests of U.S. multinationals with offshore production.

Yet, the overvalued dollar undermines American industry and the productive capacity of the U.S. economy.

At the same time, U.S. trade policy fails to address the impact of strategic trade used by Japan, China, and other countries throughout Asia.

Strategic trade views trade as part of a larger policy of strategic development, or promotion of key industries seen as critical to the process of economic development.

The use of industrial policy is almost universal, whereas in Britain and in this country government support of industry is opposed on ideological grounds.

The result is that American foreign policy pursues unilateral free trade, or one-way free trade, while China and other countries support industry as a central objective of strategic trade.

This has brought the development of global imbalances, marked by China's unprecedented accumulation of foreign reserves.

China holds some $2 trillion in U.S. Treasury bonds and other dollar denominated assets.

While trade deficits undermine American industry, China's dollar reserves are used to finance the federal budget.

This is clearly a conflict of interest, in which trade deficits are ignored for the sake of political expediency.

The result is the U.S. has now been stripped of productive capacity and left with unmanageable debt.

Twin Deficits: Financing Decline

Main Points

In the early 1980s, high interest rates used to fight inflation generated high returns on U.S. investments.

This brought unprecedented flows of foreign capital into the country, and a rise in the dollar compared to foreign currencies.

As imports became less expensive, the U.S. trade deficit rose 300 percent in the four years between 1983 and 1987.

The impact created an anomaly that transformed the U.S. economy.

The value of the trade deficit is matched by corresponding flows of foreign money coming into the country.

These financial inflows allow the federal government to finance budget deficits using foreign capital.

This system of twin deficits is the basis for the model of debt driven growth we call the New Economy.

A key development that transformed the global economy began with the historic increase in U.S. interest rates put in place to fight inflation in the late 1970s and early 1980s.

High interest rates attracted unprecedented flows of foreign money into the country, seeking high returns on U.S. investments.

This influx of foreign money caused the dollar to rise in value in relation to other currencies.

The rise in the dollar also made imports less expensive, sparking a 300 percent increase in the trade deficit between 1983 and 1987.

An unexpected side effect was the discovery that the federal government could run budget deficits without the economic consequences of inflation.

Traditionally, government deficits tend to "crowd out" the private sector.

This means government borrowing can absorb so much money that the demand for money goes up, causing inflation.

In the mid-1980s it seemed miraculous that in spite of large budget deficits, there was no shortage of capital, and hence no inflationary impact.

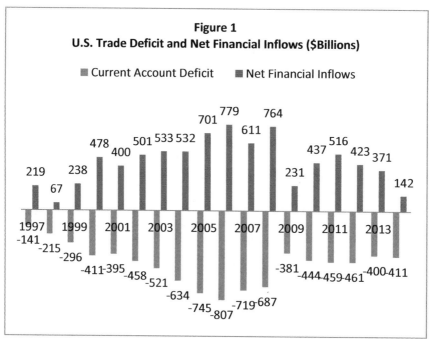

Figure 1
U.S. Trade Deficit and Net Financial Inflows ($Billions)

Source: Bureau of Economic Analysis. This figure shows the Current Account deficit, commonly referred to as the trade deficit. See the discussion on Balance of Payments in the Appendix. Financial inflow figures shown include derivatives beginning in 2009.

This came about because the balance of payments system works differently for the U.S. than for any other country in the world.

The international reserve currency is the U.S. dollar, because oil and most other commodities are paid for in dollars.

If a country can run a trade surplus with the U.S., it can use the dollars earned from trade to pay for the oil it has to import.

The result for the U.S., only because of its unique place in the system, is that trade deficits bring money into the country, which is then used to finance budget deficits.

In summary form, when the U.S. runs a trade deficit, it takes on foreign debt to finance that deficit.

When another country runs a trade surplus, it has to buy dollar denominated assets to invest that surplus.

In essence, the method of investing a foreign trade surplus is the mirror image of financing a U.S. trade deficit.

Figure 1 shows U.S. trade deficits, as well as inflows of foreign capital that offset those deficits.

The twin deficits mechanism is the driver of export led growth in the developing world, and the cause of runaway trade deficits in this country.

When budget deficits can be financed without inflation, there are no short term consequences.

As a result, there is no incentive to make the politically unpopular move of raising taxes to balance the budget.

This is a structural problem that serves political expediency, and has supported the model of debt driven growth driving the New Economy since the 1980s.

Presidents from Reagan to Obama have run the country through this twin deficit system, by financing deficits with the sale of dollar assets to trade surplus countries.

The trade deficit creates financial inflows that hide the extent of artificial growth based on debt and cheap imports, and hides the decline in the underlying economy that results.

This means the trade deficit is essentially a system of debt driven trade that provides a temporary stimulus to the economy.

Temporary stimulus makes it hard to see the extent of stagnation in the underlying economy, caused by the long term decline in productive investment that results from the trade deficit.

Benjamin Friedman wrote about the twin deficits in the mid-1980s, and described the mechanism as equivalent to the U.S. consuming its own seed corn.

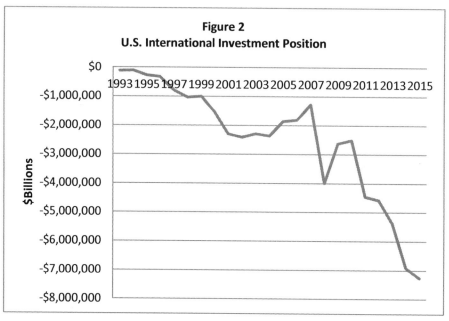

Source: Bureau of Economic Analysis.

That description is apt, because the unprecedented accumulation of debt and foreign claims on U.S. assets are used to support consumption.

There are all kinds of legitimate reasons to incur long term debt for investment.

But the U.S. has acquired historic levels of debt and sold off trillions in assets because Americans consume more than we produce.

The International Investment Position is a measure of the economy's external assets and liabilities.

Figure 2 shows the U.S. International Investment Position, which reflects a negative figure of $7.2 trillion dollars.

This means foreign ownership of U.S. assets is larger by $7.2 trillion than are U.S. claims on foreign assets.

This decline is the consequence of trade deficits and the matching inflows of foreign capital invested in U.S. assets.

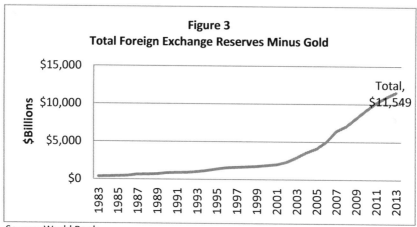

Figure 3
Total Foreign Exchange Reserves Minus Gold

Source: World Bank

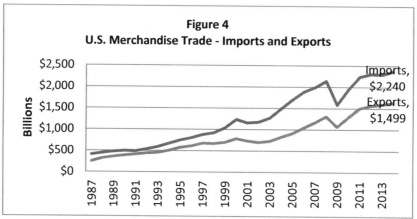

Figure 4
U.S. Merchandise Trade - Imports and Exports

U.S. Census Bureau

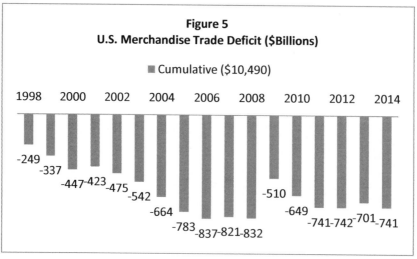

Figure 5
U.S. Merchandise Trade Deficit ($Billions)

Source: U.S. Census Bureau

Central Bank Intervention

Foreign central banks buy dollar assets to protect the exchange value of their currencies.

Large U.S. trade deficits create a flood of dollars overseas, as Americans pay in dollars for foreign goods.

This large outflow of dollars could cause a fall in the exchange value of the dollar.

Between 2000 and 2008 foreign central banks added more than $5.3 trillion in exchange reserves for this reason.

Figure 3 shows total reserves of foreign exchange have grown from less than $2 trillion in 2000 to over $11.5 trillion in 2013.

Foreign central banks have increased the supply of domestic currency (by printing it), and used the new money to buy dollar assets.

This keeps foreign currency values low and maintains parity with the dollar exchange rate.

The result has been excessive dollar liquidity that keeps interest rates low and contributes to credit bubbles.

Trade Deficits

Both political parties promote trade as a way to increase exports. But exports don't tell the whole story.

Exports create jobs, while imports drive unemployment, low domestic demand, and more off-shoring.

What we hear about are the benefits of increasing exports, while the damage done by the trade deficit is ignored.

We have a trade deficit because we import more than we export.

Because offshoring has undermined U.S. productive capacity, expanded trade means imports will always grow faster than exports.

Figure 4 shows the annual value of imports and exports.

As shown in Figure 5, from 1998 through 2014 the cumulative difference between the two was over $10 trillion dollars.

If that $10 trillion had been spent domestically, the economy would have lost a lot less than the $15+ trillion previously mentioned in the discussion on slow and distorted growth.

In 2015 the U.S. ran a non-petroleum goods deficit of some $650 billion dollars, because American manufacturing capacity has been exported.

Trade deals will do nothing to reduce that $650 billion a year deficit, and thanks to off-shoring, will actually make it worse.

Demand leakage from imports and investment leakage from off-shoring means we lose more jobs from imports than we gain from exports.

Trying to create jobs through exports is like picking up a bucket that has holes in the bottom and trying to fill it up with water.

But politicians listen to lobbyists, and lobbyists tend to represent export oriented businesses that still make things in this country.

The reality is, until we address the problem of leakage caused by the trade deficit, the economy will remain stagnant.

New Terms of Engagement
The American consumer economy relies on imports that create trade deficits.

Those trade deficits bring corresponding inflows of foreign capital that are used to purchase U.S. assets and finance debt.

The federal government is able to run large budget deficits because foreign capital is used to finance the debt.

This twin deficits mechanism has changed the terms of trade between the U.S. and other countries, and also changed the role of finance in the global economy.

While the relationship between America and the world has changed, policies that established the basis for that change have been promoted without regard to the consequences for the U.S. economy.

Instead, policy has been hijacked by ideology.

The federal government has pursued policies that have undermined American manufacturing and destroyed the industrial base of the U.S. economy.

At the same time, U.S. policy has undermined the demand generating process in this country and in every national economy in the world.

Far from the promise of shared prosperity, the global economy now serves multinational business and financial interests.

Those interests are served in ways that undermine economic development, and limit the ability of national governments to manage their own economies.

Food for Thought

The balance of payments system is an accounting system used to balance the international accounts—inflows and outflows of everything of value—of every country in the world.

The international reserve currency is the U.S. dollar, because oil and most other commodities are paid for in dollars.

Because the dollar is the reserve currency, if another country runs a trade surplus with the U.S., it has to buy dollar denominated assets to invest that surplus.

What that means for the U.S. is that trade deficits are matched by inflows of foreign capital.

This unique position of the U.S. in the international system allows the federal government to finance deficits with foreign money.

Because trade deficits are used to finance the budget deficit, this practice is known as the system of twin deficits.

This means a U.S. trade deficit of $700 billion will generate inflows of $700 billion in foreign capital.

Those financial inflows have been used to finance the federal budget deficit, by every president since the Reagan administration.

This system of twin deficits makes it possible to run annual budget deficits without raising taxes.

Because there are no short term consequences, politicians have avoided making the politically unpopular move of raising taxes to balance the budget.

But over time, political expediency in the short term has generated a cumulative burden of historic proportions.

Between 1986 and 2014, the U.S. ran cumulative trade deficits of more than $10 trillion dollars.

That means over and above the value of exports, Americans spent $10 trillion on imports, instead of on domestic goods that support U.S. jobs.

Figure 6
Offshoring

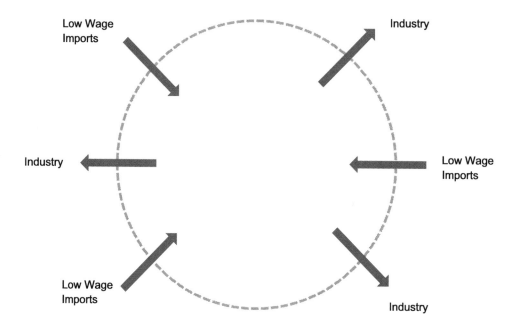

Export Manufacturing Capability

Globalism and Globalization

Main Points

In the century after the civil war, industrial development transformed America through a process of national economic integration.

Value added in manufacturing generated profit that became the basis for rising wages.

In turn, rising wages created the demand for goods that drove industrial expansion and national economic development.

At the same time, a critical element of America's growth was the use of high tariffs to protect infant industries from cheap imports.

In the same period that marked the nation's rise as an industrial power, America was the most protectionist country in the world.

It was only after World War II that free trade became the guiding principle of American foreign policy.

After the war, U.S. security interests were considered more important than the country's balance of trade.

America was the world's dominant industrial power at the time, and could afford to use trade as a subsidy for post war reconstruction in Europe and Japan.

Since the 1980s, trade has been transformed by the globalization of production.

Globalization is a process, driven by
- lower transportation costs, combined with advances in communications, and
- offshoring of manufacturing technology

Offshoring has created production platforms in low wage countries, from which consumer products are exported to markets in this country and Europe.

Globalism promotes global economic integration, based on the idea that global markets for goods offer expanded potential for growth.

But the meaning of trade has been transformed by offshoring.

Offshoring involves
- moving American manufacturing to low wage countries, and
- selling low wage products back into the American market

More than half of world trade today takes place between production facilities of multinational companies.

Since the 1980s, the political movement to deregulate industry *has been hijacked* by globalist ideology that promotes offshoring.

As a result, the U.S. economy has been stripped of productive capacity, and is now at risk of irreversible decline.

This section will clarify several points of confusion about patterns of world trade and the process of globalization.

Globalization refers to the spread of advanced technology and manufacturing capability around the world.

The forces that drive the process of globalization are
- lower transportation costs, combined with advances in communications, and
- offshoring of manufacturing technology

The evolution of instant communication through the internet and lower costs of transportation are natural developments that have facilitated offshoring.

But offshoring is fundamentally the outcome of a movement to integrate national economies into an unregulated global market.

Offshoring has transferred productive capability away from advanced economies, and created production platforms in low wage countries.

Consumer products are now made in low wage countries, and exported to markets in this country and Europe.

This globalization of production has brought increasing trade in *components* of items that are traded, as opposed to trade in finished products

More than half of world trade today is trade in components, which takes place between production facilities of multinational companies.

The result is that the value added in production is no longer retained by national economies.

Globalism is an ideology.

Globalism promotes globalization as a natural and beneficial process that is integrating national economies into an unregulated global market.

The essence of the pro-globalism / anti-globalism debate centers on:
- pathways to economic development,
- whether development is fundamentally a national or a non-national project, and
- what role, if any, government should play in fostering development.

It's certainly true that a key goal of economic development is acquiring and mastering advanced technology.

But development is also a process of national economic integration, in which the higher value-added generated by advanced production becomes the basis for higher living standards.

Historically, economic development involved a long term process of creating conditions that foster demand driven growth of value-added industry.

The transition from an agrarian to an industrial economy based on manufacturing is critical to this process of development.

The reason is that the processes involved in manufacturing create much more value added than is found in other economic sectors.

That added value creates economic surplus, or profit, which in democratic societies becomes the basis for rising wages.

In turn, rising wages are essential to generating demand for the goods produced by industry.

This process is depicted in the virtuous circle of growth, in which rising wages create demand that drives growth, providing the basis for still higher wages that further stimulate demand, etcetera.

The virtuous circle of growth is also a model of national economic integration, in which economies of scale drive investment and the continuous evolution of technology in manufacturing.

This process achieves the national objective of economic development by continually expanding both industrial output and productive capacity.

Rising output, expanded capacity, and the use of advanced technology in manufacturing are the hallmarks of modern industrial society.

In contrast to the historic pattern of development as a process of *national economic integration*, globalism advocates integration into an unregulated global economy.

Lower transportation costs combined with advances in communications have provided the impetus for offshoring.

In turn, the offshoring of manufacturing has increased access to technology and spread production capability around the world.

The result has been the creation of global supply chains, in which *component production* in multiple countries has been integrated into global networks.

An example would be a computer built with components produced in Honduras, Thailand, and Taiwan, that is then completed through final assembly in China and shipped to the American market.

This example illustrates how production centers have specialized in the production of components.

In this case the global network is based on components shipped from production or assembly plants in four different countries.

This example actually shows how global network production integrates *sub-national* economies into the global economy.

Sub-national economies are those local areas where facilities for component production and assembly are found.

This new pattern of network production is fundamentally different from the historic process of industrial expansion that evolved in the process of national economic integration.

For example, American manufacturing evolved in tandem with supply chains that connected large and interwoven groups of suppliers and skilled workers throughout this country.

The production process requires extensive product supply and distribution channels that create large numbers of additional jobs related to manufacturing.

When employees spend their paychecks, that spending also has ripple effects that support even more jobs in other areas of the economy.

For every job directly involved in manufacturing, these indirect employment effects create nearly three additional jobs that are related to manufacturing.

This system of *national production* has been and continues to be dismantled, and replaced by *global network production*.

The process entails the loss of
- national value-added in production,
- loss of employment in manufacturing,
- loss of employment in supply chains, and
- loss of employment generated by re-spending in national economies.

The result has been a *decoupling* of local production centers from the national economies in which they were previously integrated.

National economic disintegration is a co-requisite of global economic integration.

The reason is that the integration of production into global networks also drives the disintegration of national economies.

For example, specialized production of auto components in certain areas of Michigan has been integrated into global networks, as part of the global supply chain.

This is a *non-national* system of production.

The specialized production of components is integrated not into the national economy, but into the global economy through supply chains.

This system of integrating local production areas into the global economy has also brought a corresponding emphasis on regional specialization.

16

For example, component production might connect free enterprise zones in four or five different countries in East Asia.

These zones are known for specialization in various components for computers, and are integrated through network production into the global market for computers.

Since the 1980s, the political movement to deregulate industry *has been hijacked* by an ideology that promotes the integration of *sub-national* economies into an unregulated global economy.

No one in 1980 could have predicted the unprecedented spread of advanced technology and manufacturing capability around the world.

Neither the Democratic president Jimmy Carter nor the Republican president Ronald Reagan pursued an agenda of dismantling America's industrial base and rebuilding it overseas.

It would be hard to argue that Democratic or Republican administrations that followed had the intention of pursuing that agenda either.

What has happened is that trade has been transformed by both the natural processes of globalization, and by the offshoring of manufacturing that transfers American technology overseas.

Both parties promote the benefits of free trade, with no mention of the fact that what trade means today is fundamentally different from what it meant in 1980.

Armies of lobbyists, backed by mainstream economists and unprecedented campaign contributions, have persuaded our politicians that free trade is essential for economic growth.

And despite all evidence to the contrary, the political elite continue to give deference to a globalist ideology that is intellectually bankrupt.

Globalist ideology, cloaked in the rhetoric of free trade, expanded with the advent of globalization in the 1980s and its dramatic acceleration in the 1990s.

In transportation the use of containers and construction of huge container ships revolutionized trade by reducing the time and expense of ocean cargo delivery.

Container ships designed to hold standardized containers that facilitate loading with cranes eliminated the need for large crews of dock workers.

Labor costs fell as loading times were reduced from days to hours, while unit costs were also lowered by the enormous capacity of container ships.

Deregulation of airlines transformed carriers like Fedex and UPS through cost reductions that brought expanded offerings for express service and world-wide delivery.

Widespread adoption of computers in the 1980s was followed by commercial use of the internet with development of the browser in the mid-1990s.

The internet revolutionized communication by creating digital forms of information that could be delivered electronically.

Finally, the collapse of the Soviet Union in 1989, and the subsequent adoption of market reforms in China and India, brought three billion people into the unregulated global market in the 1990s.

This unprecedented expansion of the global labor supply has forever altered the dynamic of global competition for Western democracies.

Globalism promotes global economic integration, based on the idea that access to larger markets through trade offers expanded potential for growth.

Removing restrictions on trade in goods and services, as well as restrictions on capital flows, is therefore advocated by those who promote globalist free trade as the engine of growth.

But offshoring has forever changed the meaning of trade and global economic integration.

Offshoring is not trade, but rather a process of national economic disintegration that facilitates global network production through supply chains.

Evaluating the globalist argument requires consideration of whether the claimed benefits of global integration have been realized.

Free trade and the spread of technology have brought enormous growth in the *volume* of trade.

But this expansion of trade has done nothing to further the process of economic development.

Quite the contrary, unrestricted trade has brought national economic decline.

Production in multiple countries has severed the linkages between productive enterprise, democratic government, and national sovereignty.

Free Trade Origins
Virtually every country making the transition from agrarian to industrial society has done so through protectionism and the use of industrial policy to promote infant industries.

The precursor to the industrial revolution in England was the use of export duties in the 15th and 16th centuries, followed by tariffs in the 17th through the 19th centuries, enacted to develop and protect the textile industry.

Comprehensive use of industrial policy came with a 1721 law that promoted "the exportation of manufactured goods and the importation of foreign raw material."

The law raised tariffs on manufactured imports, and also provided subsidies on manufactured exports.

In the same period the newly discovered process of making steel was outlawed in the colonies, to encourage American exports of pig iron used in British steel mills.

At the same time, subsidies were established on raw material exports from America, while British import tariffs on raw materials were abolished.

It was only after the long term growth of industry behind tariff walls that British manufacturers began promoting free trade in the 19th century.

By 1860 the unquestioned supremacy of British industry had led to complete abolition of tariffs.

Britain had undergone a philosophical transformation, in which free trade was now promoted as the guiding principle of international relations.

In similar fashion, the U.S. was the most protectionist country in the world as America became the greatest industrial power ever seen.

Free trade became a guiding principle of U.S. policy only after World War II, at a time when American industry dominated the world economy.

The American System
After ratification of the U.S. constitution in 1789, the first legislation signed by George Washington was The Tariff Act, imposing a general tariff of 9 percent.

Tariffs on manufactures were later raised to 12.5 percent, and then to 25 percent at the outset of the War of 1812.

Support for higher tariffs grew when British imports flooded the market after the War of 1812.

The Tariff Act of 1816 imposed duties of 30 percent on iron imports and 25 percent on cotton and woolens.

The movement was led by Henry Clay, who like Alexander Hamilton wanted an American System of trade that would use tariffs to protect infant industry, and use tariff revenue to build infrastructure such as canals and railroads.

In 1824 import tariffs were raised to 35 percent on iron, wool, and hemp, but were criticized by Northern manufacturers as being too low.

Duties were raised to almost 62 percent in 1828, but were vehemently opposed by Southern planters, who traded cotton for British imports.

Ultimately the Republican Party, formed in 1854, adopted a platform that combined the American System with federal land grants (The Homestead Act) for Western settlers.

In 1860 support from Western states brought the election of Abraham Lincoln, who had supported the American System since the 1830s.

Tariffs were raised repeatedly during the Civil War, and stayed between 40 percent and 50 percent thereafter, until Democrats won the presidency more than 50 years after the 1860 election.

These tariff rates made the U.S. the most protectionist country in the world, while in the same period American workers earned the highest wages in the world.

Between 1870 and 1913
- wages rose 53 percent,
- national income grew 500 percent,
- industrial output rose 5 percent per year
- national income per capita doubled, and
- the economy grew at more than 4 percent per year

When Democrats won the presidency in 1913, the average tariff on manufactures was lowered from 44 percent to 25 percent.

Woodrow Wilson's presidency spanned U.S. involvement in World War I (1917-1919), which re-directed industry to wartime production.

Yet despite substantial increase in government spending, gross national product in real (inflation adjusted) terms was only 13 percent higher in 1918 than in 1913.

After Republicans returned to power in 1921, tariffs were raised by 40 percent compared to the 1913-1920 period.

The average rate imposed by the Forney-McCumber tariff was 37 percent, and was followed by the economic boom of the roaring twenties.

Between 1922 and 1928
- industrial production rose 70 percent,
- factory output per hour rose 75 percent,
- gross national product rose 40 percent, and
- national income per capita rose 30 percent

From 1923 to 1929 corporate profits rose 62 percent, while worker incomes only rose between 8 percent and 11 percent.

Despite inequality in the gains from growth, this was an extraordinary level of vitality for an economy with an average 37 percent tariff.

While pent up demand during the war fed the post war boom, tariffs channeled that demand into driving economic growth domestically, not higher spending on imports.

Unlike the American economy today, there was far less leakage of demand from buying imports in the 1920s.

Trade and International Security
U.S. promotion of free trade since the end of World War II represents a complete reversal of the high tariff policy that protected infant industry and brought the historic rise of American manufacturing.

Much like Britain in the 19th century, the U.S. only began promoting free trade after America's rise to a position of world dominance in the post war period.

A turning point for this watershed change in policy was the political debate over the Smoot-Hawley tariff passed in 1930.

In 1928 Herbert Hoover campaigned on a platform of higher tariffs for agricultural products, to protect farmers.

But the bill passed by Congress in 1929 increased tariffs across the board to 48 percent, some 30 percent higher than the Forney - McCumber tariff.

Despite the fact Smoot-Hawley wasn't signed into law until June 1930, Democrats in the 1932 election blamed the tariff for the onset of the Depression, winning the presidency for Franklin Roosevelt.

While there is a widely held and somewhat generalized view that Smoot-Hawley may have worsened the Depression, the actual evidence is far from conclusive.

First, while U.S. imports from Europe fell by two thirds, only half of those imports were actually subject to tariffs.

Moreover, imports of goods that were duty free actually declined more than the imports that were subject to tariffs.

Because the money supply declined by one third and credit virtually disappeared, a more likely explanation for the fall in imports was the decline of incomes and loss of available credit to buy anything at all.

The level of U.S. imports fell dramatically in 2009, which is easily attributed to falling demand after the 2008 financial crisis and recession that followed.

This fall in imports, without any tariff to blame, supports the conclusion that imports fall when demand falls, not that imports fell during the Depression because of Smoot-Hawley.

Conversely, when demand was high, as in the period after 37 percent tariffs were imposed under Forney-McCumber (1922 – 1928), imports soared and the economy boomed.

High tariffs imposed by other countries in retaliation against Smoot-Hawley have also been cited as contributing to the fall in world trade and thereby exacerbating the Depression.

Yet some tariffs other countries imposed were actually passed before Smoot-Hawley, and reflected domestic political debate that made little mention of retaliation against this country.

Most important of all is the fact that at the outset of the Depression, trade accounted for less than 10 percent of U.S. GDP.

It isn't logical to argue that the entire economy shrank by 47 percent, because trade declined in a sector that accounted for less than 1/10th of the economy overall.

Furthermore, while Smoot-Hawley was replaced by the 1934 Reciprocal Trade Agreements Act, the Depression continued for another six years.

The 1934 Trade Act gave the president the power to reduce tariffs on goods from any country by 50 percent, provided reciprocal tariff reductions were agreed by the country involved.

In one of the most sophisticated studies of the period, Smoot-Hawley was found to have a slightly negative impact on the world economy, and a slightly positive impact on the U.S. economy.

Factors that did prolong the Depression include the dramatic fall in the money supply, as well as Roosevelt pre-maturely raising taxes in 1936 and reducing spending in 1937.

Yet despite all evidence to the contrary, Smoot-Hawley is continually blamed for the Depression.

In a 1993 debate over NAFTA, Vice President Al Gore gave Ross Perot a framed picture of the tariff's sponsors, who were shown shaking hands after the bill had passed.

The reality is the U.S. promoted free trade after World War II as a foreign policy tool for protecting American security interests in Europe and Asia.

Post war reconstruction in Europe and Japan was essential to offset the rise of socialist and more extreme communist movements that were widely mobilized at the time.

Preferential access to the American market was critical to reconstruction, because it provided a stable and reliable market for European and Japanese producers, above and beyond what could be sold in their home markets.

In the Cold War that escalated in the 1950s, access to the American market was used to subsidize growth in Taiwan and South Korea, and subsequently throughout Latin America as well.

This use of trade for geopolitical purposes actually bore no resemblance to free trade.

Instead, the U.S. provided access to the American market to secure alliances and promote allied industrial expansion that was considered essential to political stability.

Trade and Development
The use of trade as a tool of geopolitics was given priority in the post war period, and was marked by official U.S. policy of promoting imports from Europe and Japan.

When import competition became an issue in some sectors in the 1950s and 1960s, military security was repeatedly invoked to trump the case that the U.S. economy was being undermined.

Over time it became increasingly clear that U.S. free trade policy was competing unsuccessfully with policies of strategic trade, used to varying degrees by European countries and most successfully by Japan.

Strategic trade views trade as part of a larger policy of strategic development, or promotion of key industries seen as critical to the process of economic development.

Government sponsorship of key industries through industrial policy was central to economic development in post war Europe and Japan, and later throughout Asia as well.

In Japan the Ministry of International Trade and Industry (MITI) used tariffs and non-tariff barriers to keep foreign companies out of the domestic market, and used low cost financing and subsidies to support infant industries.

In the 1980s American companies lost market share and ultimately ceded entire industries in consumer electronics to Japanese firms.

While post war geopolitics shaped U.S. foreign policy, a profound ideological change had also evolved among decision makers regarding trade.

As the U.S. assumed the role of world leader after the war, American economists promoted free trade, following Britain's adoption of free trade in the 19th century.

Britain's decline after the mid-19th century occurred in precisely the same period as U.S. protectionism, resulting in the rise of American industry to a position of world dominance by 1913.

Historians consider unrivaled industrial supremacy as key to explaining Britain's philosophical conversion to free trade in the mid-19th century.

Thereafter, despite the extraordinary decline of manufacturing that followed, pursuit of free trade destroyed the country's industrial base and brought the fall of Britain as a world power.

Yet even with this historical lesson in plain view, U.S. policy in the 1980s was patterned on British principles of free trade and offered little response to the growing challenge from Japan.

Adhering to the belief in free markets, the U.S. refused to protect American companies that were competing with rival firms supported by the Japanese government.

U.S. policy amounted to deliberate abandonment of American companies, because the philosophy of free trade precludes government intervention in the market.

This *unilateral* adherence to free trade has been described as a trade war, in which only one side is firing the shots.

The ultimate outcome was a divergence between Japanese companies supported by MITI, and American firms that were unable to compete and were thereby forced to offshore their production.

At the same time, while the spread of technology led to network production through supply chains, the process had a much greater impact on American companies than on competing firms in Japan and other countries throughout Asia.

Network Production
and National Policy
As supplier production of components has evolved, American companies have come to specialize in design and final assembly, and ultimately to rely on multiple suppliers that specialize in components.

This restructuring process has both facilitated offshoring and led American firms to shed manufacturing operations and production.

As production value added has become increasingly globalized, U.S. multinationals have contributed less and less value to the American economy.

Between 1995 and 2005, foreign value added grew at twice the rate of domestic value added.

Consider the case of Apple, which maintains greater control over the production process than is typical for most American companies.

Apple creates software and controls production of electronic processors and hardware, while also operating retail stores that sell the company's hardware, software, and services.

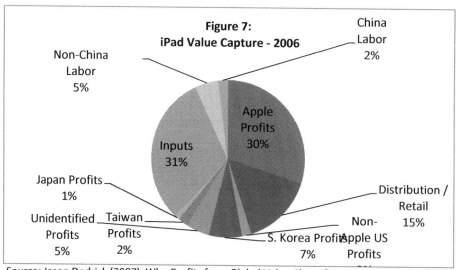

Figure 7:
iPad Value Capture - 2006

- China Labor 2%
- Non-China Labor 5%
- Apple Profits 30%
- Inputs 31%
- Japan Profits 1%
- Unidentified Profits 5%
- Taiwan Profits 2%
- S. Korea Profits 7%
- Non-Apple US Profits
- Distribution / Retail 15%

Source: Jason Dedrick (2007). Who Profits from Global Value Chains?
School of Information Studies, Syracuse University.

Figure 8
Worldwide iPod-related Jobs and Compensation, 2006

Worldwide iPod-related Jobs

	Production	Retail / Non-Professional	Engineering / Professional	Total
U.S.	30	7,789	6,101	13,290
Non-U.S.	19,160	4,824	3,265	27,250

Worldwide iPod-related Compensation

	Production	Retail / Non-Professional	Engineering / Professional	Total
U.S.	$1,429,200	$220,183,310	$562,191,318	$753,287,510
Non-U.S.	$90,236,050	$96,500,000	$131,750,000	$318,486,050

Source: Same as Figure 7

Figure 7 shows a breakdown of the value capture in the Apple iPad in 2006.

The total U.S. value captured was 47 percent.

The remaining value of the iPad reflects non-U.S. profits (15 percent), and non-U.S. production costs (38 percent).

For this country, the effect is that 53 percent of the iPad's retail value, which might otherwise have served to stimulate the economy, has been lost.

Yet sourcing a larger share of production in this country would be costly for Apple, due to higher U.S. labor costs.

Note that labor costs were only 7 percent of the iPad's retail value.

Figure 8 shows iPod related employment and compensation, and provides a breakdown of U.S. and non-U.S. characteristics and totals.

In 2006 there were 27,250 jobs outside this country involved in producing the iPod.

Annual wages paid in that non-U.S. employment came to $318 million dollars.

While there were more retail and engineering jobs in this country, 67 percent of the jobs and 30 percent of wages paid in producing the iPod were outside the U.S. economy.

Apple is only one company among untold thousands of companies engaged in global production for the American market.

The problem for the U.S., and for Western democracies more generally, is that goods are no longer produced in the markets where they are sold.

Asian countries produce more than they consume, and as a result consistently generate annual surpluses in their international trade.

Those trade surpluses are the mirror image of trade deficits in this country.

A principle cause of the discrepancy is that global production has had far less impact on Japanese and other Asian companies than on American firms.

Strategic management designed to limit competition among Japanese companies led to Japan's dominance in computers and key technologies like machine tools in the 1980s.

Strategic management is based on the tacit agreement among Japanese producers to rely on Japanese suppliers and distributors, as part of a coherent strategy to promote Japanese control of key markets.

This pronounced feature of national identity on the part of Japanese companies has no counterpart in how production is organized by U.S. multinationals.

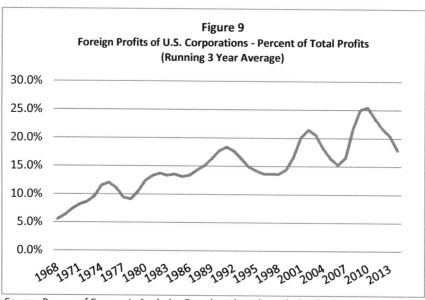

Figure 9
Foreign Profits of U.S. Corporations - Percent of Total Profits
(Running 3 Year Average)

Source: Bureau of Economic Analysis. Based on data through the third
quarter of 2014.

American firms focus on price and quality, but disregard the national identity of component suppliers.

The result is that collectively, Japanese companies capture a larger share of value added and thereby serve the national interests of their home country by expanding national wealth.

The same is true throughout Asia, where strategic trade and industrial policy are promoted as rational self-interest, and aid the process of economic development and national economic integration.

The opposite policy orientation in this country is ideological and irrational.

The result has been disintegration of the U.S. economy, because promoting consumption is considered more important than supporting the development of productive enterprise.

Offshoring is Not Trade

The primary trading relationships in the world today are adversarial.

China and other countries throughout Asia practice strategic trade.

For China, strategic trade is a directed policy to first acquire American manufacturing capability, and then out-compete the U.S. with technology and know-how gained in the process.

Second, offshoring has transformed the meaning of trade.

Manufacturing has been offshored to low wage countries to produce goods for export to Western countries – to the very countries where industry was previously located.

In essence, offshoring is the reverse of economic development.

Yet those who defend offshoring invoke the supposed benefits of free trade, and embrace the idea that it makes no difference whether the U.S. exports "computer chips or potato chips."

This expression embodies the idea that the U.S. can thrive as a service economy.

It is more common to hear reference to the idea that the U.S. is shedding old economy industries, and is specializing in advanced technologies of the New Economy.

In reality the U.S. has been running trade deficits in high technology products since the mid-1990s.

Figure 9 shows the increasing proportion of corporate profits derived from foreign operations, rising from 5 percent in the 1960s, to an average 22 percent since 2008.

At the same time, in this country net fixed non-residential investment declined from an average over 4.5 percent of GDP in the late 1960s, to only 2 percent of GDP in 2013.

While other countries practice strategic trade, the U.S. practices unilateral, one-way free trade.

Countries that successfully manage global integration are those that practice strategic trade.

Unilateral free trade is the official U.S. policy of industrial suicide.

Offshoring is a process of transferring American technology to foreign countries through global supply chains.

In the West and in much of the developing world, the only winners are the multinational business and financial interests that have rigged the system to their advantage.

Food for Thought

Offshoring and the production of components through global supply chains have created *non-national* systems of production.

Globalism promotes integration into an unregulated global market as being mutually beneficial for the countries involved.

In reality, the loss of national production results in the loss of
- national value-added in production,
- loss of employment in manufacturing,
- loss of employment in supply chains, and
- loss of employment generated by re-spending in national economies.

National systems of production have been dismantled and replaced with network production through global supply chains.

Offshoring is not trade, but rather a process of national economic disintegration that facilitates global network production through supply chains.

For this country and Western democracies more generally, *offshoring is the reverse of economic development.*

China, Japan, and other countries throughout Asia devote government funding to protect key industries based on principles of strategic trade.

Strategic trade views trade as part of a larger policy of strategic development, or promotion of key industries seen as critical to the process of economic development.

Strategic trade promotes industrial policy as rational self-interest, to aid the process of economic development.

Offshoring has brought the transfer of manufacturing technology and capacity from this country to China and other countries throughout Asia.

The reason is that U.S. policy is captive to globalist ideology, promoted by multinational business and financial interests that have no loyalty to this country.

Summary

In the international system, the reserve currency is the U.S. dollar, because oil and most commodities are paid for in dollars.

The result for the U.S., only because of its unique place in the system, is that trade deficits bring money into the country, which is used to finance budget deficits.

The dollar's role as reserve currency is essentially a guarantee that financial inflows will be the mirror image of the trade deficit.

Those financial inflows hide the extent of artificial growth based on debt and cheap imports, as well as the decline in the underlying economy that results.

At the same time, the Twin Deficits mechanism has changed the terms of trade between the U.S. and other countries as well as the role of finance in the global economy.

The twin deficits mechanism is the driver of export led growth in the developing world, and also the cause of unprecedented accumulation of debt in this country.

This is a structural problem that serves political expediency and has sustained the model of debt driven growth since the 1980s.

Because financial inflows serve to sustain the New Economy model of growth, policy makers have adopted a view of trade deficits as being harmless.

This view supports the idea that the globalization of production is a natural outcome of technological change.

But there is nothing natural or inevitable in the trend toward global production.

Countries practicing strategic trade have been far less affected by the process of globalization than is true in this country.

Offshoring has transformed the meaning of trade.

Prior to the rise of off-shoring, global economic integration referred to free trade among countries, which served to integrate national economies into the global market.

But today global networks undermine the national value-added in manufacturing production.

This brings large scale loss of employment that would otherwise be generated through supply chains and the impact of re-spending throughout national economies.

The result has been to sever the link between local production centers and the national economies in which they were previously integrated.

*With the transformation of trade by offshoring, **national** economic disintegration has become a co-requisite of **global** economic integration.*

The reason is that the integration of production into global networks also drives the disintegration of national economies.

Official U.S. policy facilitates off-shoring and exacerbates national economic decline.

The Wall Street / Trade Complex

Beginning in the 1980s, Wall Street rules—changes in both business practices and legislation—created fundamental changes in American business.

The shareholder value revolution brought the granting of stock options to corporate executives and an exclusive emphasis on short term profits.

In the 1980s the impact was corporate restructuring through mergers and acquisitions that were accompanied by downsizing and layoffs.

In the 1990s Wall Street influence in the Treasury Department and the IMF resulted in the use of U.S. foreign policy as another tool of corporate restructuring.

Following a series of booms fueled by international lending, economic collapse in Mexico and later throughout Asia unfolded in debt crisis.

The response orchestrated by officials in the Treasury Department was to provide IMF loan guarantees that
- bailed out Western banks,
- devalued the currencies of debtor countries, and
- imposed requirements for economic restructuring designed to ensure repayment of loans.

Economic restructuring was designed to reduce consumption as a way to guarantee debtor countries would build up trade surpluses with the United States.

Debtor countries could then use the dollars earned from trade surpluses to pay off loans.

The effect was to expand the incentive for U.S. multinationals to raise profits through offshoring.

The incentive to offshore production to low wage countries was now reinforced by IMF bailouts that brought devaluation and further reduced the cost of labor.

Driven by the goal of maximizing profits to raise share prices, U.S. multinationals shut down manufacturing in this country and moved production overseas.

Offshoring brought decline of American manufacturing and explosion of the U.S. trade deficit, matched by record profits for Wall Street and U.S. multinational companies.

This Wall Street/Trade complex has made billions in profits from offshoring, at the expense of American industry and the U.S. economy.

Offshoring has also been aided by incentives from foreign governments, especially China, which makes it impossible for American manufacturing to compete.

Yet there has been virtually no response from successive administrations in both parties.

The reason is that the U.S. trade deficit with China brings matching inflows of foreign capital from China of more than $300 billion a year.

Perversely, the U.S. trade deficit generates the inflow of foreign capital required to finance the federal budget deficit.

The end result is a conflict of interest, in which the federal government represents multinational business and financial interests that undermine American industry and the U.S. economy.

Main Points

In the 1970s, high oil prices created an excess of Middle East export revenue.

These revenues were denominated in dollars, and became known as petrodollars.

Petrodollar investments drove exponential growth of international lending, creating economic booms in developing countries.

In the late 1970s, the continued rise in oil prices brought high U.S. interest rates, imposed as anti-inflation policy.

In the 1980s, economic booms driven by international lending collapsed, resulting in debt crisis.

This brought IMF bailouts, in the form of loans for crisis countries, which were used to pay off debts to U.S. and other Western banks.

At the same time, the condition of IMF assistance was the acceptance of economic reforms designed to reduce consumption.

This restructuring created a surplus of trade for debtor countries, generating foreign exchange that was needed for loan payments.

In the 1990s, the condition of IMF assistance included removal of restrictions on capital flows, creating unprecedented foreign investment that drove economic booms throughout Asia.

Asian economies were driven by export led growth, based on production of consumer goods for the American market.

In the mid-1990s, the pursuit of this strategy by multiple countries brought a decline in economic growth, and a corresponding loss of export earnings.

Economic booms driven by international lending collapsed, resulting in debt crisis.

This brought a new round of bailouts, with unprecedented sums provided through IMF loans.

The result was a series of currency devaluations for debtor countries.

These devaluations supported the continued production of consumer goods for the American market.

Officials at the IMF and the U.S. Treasury engineered devaluation of developing country currencies.

This policy supports the model of export led growth in the developing world, which exacerbates offshoring and undermines U.S. manufacturing.

The Rise of Global Finance

In the 1970s, high oil prices created an enormous increase in Middle East export revenue.

These dollar denominated funds were then recycled through loans made to Western governments, and to developing countries.

This surge of international lending drove the first wave of inter-related processes that have since come to be called financial globalization.

By the early 1980s, international markets were valued at $1.5 trillion, nearly ten times their 1973 value of $160 billion.

In the same period, lending rose to $300 billion a year, close to ten times the 1973 level of $35 billion.

By the early 1990s, international markets controlled some $5 trillion in assets, and provided over $1 trillion a year in loans.

Ironically, high oil prices were a fundamental cause of economic stagnation in the 1970s.

Yet one outcome of slower growth was a widespread need to run budget deficits, which could now be financed through petrodollar loans.

For developing countries, expanded lending brought financing for investments needed to aid the growth of industry.

John Perkins has described the pattern of infrastructure development promoted in the 1970s by the World Bank.

Perkins served as a consultant on a range of infrastructure projects approved for World Bank development loans.

Projects typically involved transportation (ports, highways, and airports), as well as hydroelectric dams and construction of infrastructure for electricity and other utilities.

Perkins describes loan approvals based on inflated projections of future growth rates, with the projects completed through contracts awarded to American companies.

When growth projections were later found to be overstated, the governments of the countries involved were unable to generate the tax revenue needed to repay the loans.

While development projects often had unfortunate outcomes, the process unfolded over a long period, with private sector loans following on the heels of government loans from the World Bank and other multilateral agencies.

Ultimately, the result of excessive lending was the creation of a series of economic booms, which ultimately ended in collapse.

In 1979, another rise in oil prices further raised the cost of manufactured imports, while high U.S. interest rates drove rates on new loans higher, and increased the cost of debt service.

During the 1980s, more than 30 countries accepted rescue packages from the International Monetary Fund (IMF), made necessary by destabilizing effects of petrodollar loans.

In every case the IMF intervened to prevent default, by providing government loans that were used to pay off debts to private sector banks.

At the same time, the condition of IMF assistance was that debtor countries implement a coordinated set of market reforms and austerity programs.

These measures followed the logic of using free trade and deregulation to integrate national economies into the unregulated global market.

Economic Restructuring
Structural adjustment programs were established as conditions required by the IMF for new loans, and for rolling over existing loans.

Reflecting the extent of U.S. influence within the IMF, these conditions became known collectively as the Washington Consensus.

IMF conditions include:
Monetary austerity – impose high interest rates as a means of attracting investment and stabilizing the currency

Fiscal austerity – increase tax revenue and reduce government spending

Privatization – sell state-owned enterprises (public utilities) to reduce government spending

Deregulation - reduce environmental and labor regulations, and remove price controls

Financial liberalization – remove restrictions on
- cross border flows of foreign capital, and
- foreign ownership of banks and other businesses

Trade liberalization – reduce
- Import tariffs, and
- government subsidies

Export expansion – reduce restrictions on foreign companies, to encourage greater production of exports needed for foreign exchange

The stated objective of adjustment programs was to enable debtor countries to generate foreign exchange needed to pay back loans.

Ironically, excessive lending and the pursuit of export led growth were key characteristics of economies that collapsed in debt crisis.

Yet, IMF conditions place even greater emphasis on promoting exports as a means of earning the foreign exchange needed for debt service.

Impact of Restructuring
Austerity calls for reduced spending on subsidies that support domestic development.

Developing countries have reduced funding on irrigation projects and subsidies for small farmers, while promoting export agriculture that tends to be dominated by multinational companies.

For example, 50 percent of genetically modified food (GMF) crops are grown in developing countries.

These GMF varieties have higher yields, and are used as export crops that generate the foreign exchange needed for loan servicing.

But multinationals control three quarters of GMF patents, while the countries where the crops are grown suffer increasing poverty and a loss of national control over agriculture.

At the same time, there are large agricultural subsidies in all the member states of the European Union, as well as U.S. subsidies of more than $20 billion a year to agriculture.

The requirement for liberalized trade also provides sharp contrast with the use of tariffs in the U.S. and other advanced countries, throughout their respective periods of industrialization.

Just as tariffs were used in Britain and in this country to protect infant industry, all the industrial democracies were thoroughly protectionist when their own industries were being established.

Trade liberalization and removal of restrictions on foreign ownership makes it impossible to protect domestic industry from competition with multinational companies.

IMF adjustment programs ignore this history, and fail to acknowledge different stages of development in poor countries.

This double standard undermines the long term interests of this country, by slowing development of consumer markets for U.S. products.

Another aspect of adjustment programs intended to make debtor countries better able to pay back loans, is the requirement to raise interest rates.

The result is that returns on investment are much higher in the developing world, than are comparable investments in this country.

High rates undermine local producers and businesses, just as high interest rates hurt consumers and small business in this country.

Local businesses are less able to withstand the higher cost of credit, and more vulnerable to being acquired by multinationals that have been freed of restrictions on foreign ownership.

At the same time, financial liberalization has brought unprecedented inflows of foreign capital, encouraging speculation and increasing the likelihood of boom and bust cycles.

Without restrictions, foreign capital creates instability by generating huge inflows of money that quickly flow outward in times of crisis.

Boom and bust cycles lead to banking crises and further bailouts, which serve to perpetuate the cycle and increase the overall supply of money in the system.

This excess liquidity feeds the rise of speculation, which particularly in respect to commodities has greatest impact on the poorest segment of the population.

Between 2005 and 2008, the price of maize nearly tripled, with prices increasing for rice by 170 percent, and for wheat by over 125 percent.

Speculation is driven by large investors, who periodically delay the entry of commodity stocks into the market.

The impact of speculation in the oil market is also substantial.

Estimates range from a low between 50 and 80 cents per gallon of gas, to a high of more than $2 dollars per gallon.

Higher estimates reflect speculation that is undoubtedly occurring in the unregulated derivatives market, which is not subject to reporting requirements.

To whatever extent speculation occurs, clearly those with the lowest incomes suffer the most when commodity prices rise.

The excessive cost of food and fuel also reduces demand for everything else, to the detriment of the national economy overall.

Global Business and
U.S. Foreign Policy
In one respect IMF austerity programs look like another case of policy that is rational in one context becoming irrational in another.

The economies of Latin American countries involved in the debt crisis of the 1980s were characterized by high inflation.

High oil prices increased the cost of manufactured imports, while high interest rates increased debt payments on new loans needed to finance trade deficits.

IMF austerity measures implemented at the time had the effect of inducing recession by use of high interest rates and cuts in government spending.

While there is much to criticize about the impact of austerity policies in the 1980s, policies designed to bring about contraction of the economy made sense in the context of high inflation in debtor countries at the time.

In contrast, the context of the 1990s debt crisis was fundamentally different.

In the 1990s, it was the removal of restrictions on capital flows that created an oversupply of credit and economic booms, which later led to collapse and debt crisis.

Instead of inflation, the economies of crisis countries were characterized by *collapse of asset prices and deflation*, similar to what occurred during the Depression in this country.

Yet the response from the U.S. and the IMF was to insist on the same austerity programs that had been promoted in the 1980s.

This policy was utterly irrational with regard to the impact on debtor countries.

As existing recessions were made more severe, prolonged stagnation was only avoided through devaluation of debtor country currencies.

This process established the high dollar policy, which served the interests of creditors and foreign investors, but also brought an explosion of the U.S. trade deficit.

U.S. foreign policy, promoted by the Treasury Department through the IMF, has served multinational business and financial interests, at the expense of American industry.

International Institutions
and Globalist Ideology
The IMF was founded at the end of World War II, with the mission of maintaining global stability and preventing a repeat of the Great Depression.

From its founding in 1947, the IMF was centrally concerned with supporting global demand.

Specifically, the IMF was established to provide loans to countries that lacked the resources to stimulate demand during periods of recession.

The intention was to provide a mechanism for collective action at the global level, and thereby maintain international stability.

In the early 1980s, the IMF underwent a profound change in orientation, when deregulation and austerity were promoted as the new essentials for stability.

The same period saw a parallel change at the World Bank, which was established to alleviate poverty by providing loans for development projects.

With the change at the IMF, the types of loans made by the World Bank began to include structural adjustment loans.

These loans provide funding for IMF austerity programs, which limit consumption and increase poverty.

Richard Peet describes the IMF, the World Bank, and the World Trade Organization (WTO) as an unholy trinity, which has undermined growth and reversed decades of progress, throughout the developing world.

The U.S. is the largest donor to both the World Bank and the IMF, and is the only IMF member country with veto power.

The Reagan administration marked a change in personnel appointed to represent the U.S., which brought a corresponding change in policy.

IMF officials were selected from the financial community, promoted policies that served financial interests, and ultimately returned to prestigious careers in the financial sector.

This kind of revolving door came to apply equally to the role of policy makers at the Treasury Department in this country.

Likewise, just as promotion of the New Economy has been described as fully bipartisan, IMF policies that originated in the 1980s have been maintained, with few exceptions, ever since.

A key feature of the New Economy in this country has been the promotion of financial capital over productive industry.

In parallel, the IMF has promoted the interests of creditors, at the expense of economic development.

Bailing out Creditors

The initial IMF response to debt crisis is to put up billions of dollars to keep exchange rates at unrealistically high levels.

This creates a short period marked by capital flight.

Foreign investors and wealthy people are able to move money out of the country before the exchange rate falls.

IMF loans are provided to governments in poor countries.

Governments provide assistance to domestic banks, which then use the money to pay off private debts.

Once private sector debt has been nationalized, the currency is devalued, and the country is left with high unemployment and restrictions on government spending.

Anti-inflation Policy and Slow Growth

The IMF has insisted on very high interest rates, which attract foreign investment, but which also serve to reduce domestic consumption.

In a country with low inflation, low consumption creates a trade surplus.

IMF conditions include high interest rates, because low consumption creates the trade surplus needed to earn dollars.

This is why the IMF focuses exclusively on financial variables in a country's balance of payments.

In essence, the IMF requires restructuring of national economies to generate revenue that can be used for debt service.

The result is high unemployment and distorted growth in the underlying economy.

At the same time, trade surpluses in poor countries act as a mirror image of the trade deficit in this country.

High Dollar Policy

In the early 1980s, high interest rates created record trade deficits.

Between 1985 and 1987, the U.S. dollar was devalued by 50 percent, relative to the Japanese yen and the German mark.

This lower value kept trade deficits under two percent of GDP through the mid-1990s.

Thereafter, the Mexican peso crisis brought an unprecedented $20 billion commitment from the U.S. to prevent default.

After an orchestrated bailout of the banks, the peso was devalued by 70 percent in relation to the dollar.

As a result, the U.S. balance of trade with Mexico went from a surplus of $1.7 billion in 1993, to a deficit of $17.5 billion in 1996.

Over the next decade, the peso lost another 43 percent of its dollar value, creating a U.S. trade deficit with Mexico of $64 billion in 2008.

The Asian financial crisis of 1997 followed a similar pattern.

A series of credit-fueled booms unfolded throughout Asia in the late 1980s.

Thereafter, the region experienced impressive annual growth rates between six percent and eight percent in the first half of the 1990s.

Asian banks borrowed from international lenders, and then loaned the money to finance domestic business.

Unfortunately, loans from international lenders had short maturities, whereas financing for domestic business was provided through long term loans.

As the boom was cresting in 1996, export growth slowed because countries throughout Asia were pursuing the same model of export-led development.

The result was a shortage of the dollars needed to make loan payments to foreign banks.

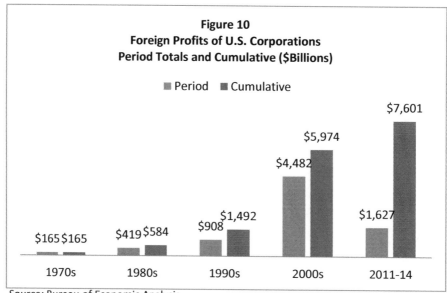

Figure 10
Foreign Profits of U.S. Corporations
Period Totals and Cumulative ($Billions)

■ Period ■ Cumulative

Source: Bureau of Economic Analysis.

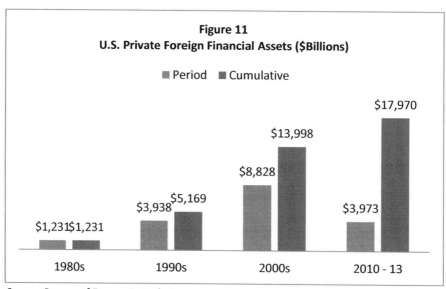

Figure 11
U.S. Private Foreign Financial Assets ($Billions)

■ Period ■ Cumulative

Source: Bureau of Economic Analysis.

Once it became clear what was happening, traders began to view exchange rates throughout the region as being overvalued.

As speculators bid down the value of local currencies, domestic banks ran out of dollars and became insolvent.

IMF bailouts were followed by devaluations in the range of 46 percent – 50 percent for Thailand, Indonesia, and South Korea.

In each case the U.S. balance of trade with these countries went from surplus to deficit.

Devaluation allowed debtor countries to repay loans by building up trade surpluses with the U. S., causing an explosion of our trade deficit.

As a percentage of GDP, the U.S. trade deficit went from 1.7 percent in 1997 to 2.5 percent in 1998, to 3.3 percent in 1999.

In 2000, the trade deficit broke a new record of 4.2 percent of GDP, much worse in absolute terms than the previous record set in the late 1980s.

Thereafter, the U.S. trade deficit continued to grow, and in 2006 reached a record 6.5 percent of GDP.

As the trade deficit grew, manufacturing employment declined.

Between 1998 and 2010, U.S. manufacturing lost six million jobs.

Policies imposed by the IMF protect creditors, but undermine the development of consumer markets, and thereby limit demand for U.S. exports.

At the same time, devaluation of foreign currencies makes offshoring all the more profitable.

The result is that U.S. multinationals make ever higher profits supplying cheap imports, while driving American job loss in manufacturing.

IMF bailouts and the high dollar policy serve multinational business and financial interests, at the expense of American industry and the U.S. economy.

Figure 10 shows foreign profits of U.S. corporations, which in the 2000s were nearly three times the level of profit in the 1990s.

In 2011, foreign profits of US companies were over $450 billion dollars.

Figure 11 shows U.S. private foreign financial assets.

Private foreign financial assets in the 1990s were nearly three times that of the 1980s.

In the 2000s, the value rose to nearly twice that of the 1990s.

Global Finance and the IMF Agenda

Joseph Stiglitz has written extensively on the contrast between IMF policies forced on developing countries, and domestic policy in this country.

In the 1990s, Stiglitz (as chairman of Clinton's Council of Economic Advisors) worked with Treasury Secretary Robert Rubin to defeat a proposed balanced budget amendment to the constitution.

The amendment would have forced the federal government to restrict spending to revenues, making it impossible to run budget deficits.

During recession, the business cycle enters a downturn and tax revenues fall.

The balanced budget amendment would have required cutting spending or raising taxes *during recession*, which would only make the problem worse.

One of the central lessons of the Depression was that during recession, expanded government spending is required to maintain demand.

Ironically, while the balanced budget amendment was defeated, Rubin and the Treasury department actively promoted IMF austerity measures in poor countries.

What Treasury Department officials considered bad economic policy in this country, was promoted through the IMF as a way of protecting banks.

Another contrast in policy involves the repeal of controls on foreign capital.

Following collapse of the Soviet Union, U.S. policymakers began actively promoting the removal of restrictions on capital flows.

Large foreign banks distort the market in poor countries, because the much smaller domestic banks can't compete.

Depression legislation in this country prohibited nationwide banking, until restrictions were repealed with the 1994 Interstate Banking Act, passed during the Clinton administration.

The legitimate concern was that money would flow to major financial centers like New York, and lead to greater concentration in the banking sector.

After the Interstate Banking Act became law, concentration in the U.S. banking sector rose to levels not seen since the 1920s.

Stieglitz describes the IMF's insistence on removing restrictions on foreign banks and capital flows as a clear case of special interest politics.

There is no case to be made that it was important to the U.S. national interest to promote unrestricted capital flows in developing countries.

41

In fact, capital flows were restricted in Europe and in this country until the 1970s, and were recognized in the post war period as posing an inherent danger to global economic stability.

Unrestricted capital flows bring financial instability and collapse, followed by currency devaluation that only benefits Wall Street and U.S. multinational companies.

Another policy contrast is the promotion of greater independence for central banks in developing countries.

One of the conditions of IMF assistance to South Korea was a provision to change the charter of the central bank, to make it more independent of the political process.

At the same time, in the depth of the worst crisis in the country's history, the IMF instructed South Korea's central bank to base its monetary policy exclusively on the rate of inflation.

While South Korea had no history of inflation, the cause of the financial crisis also had nothing to do with inflation.

Instead, the crisis was caused by removal of restrictions on capital flows, which ultimately pushed domestic banks into default.

Here again, there was nothing of relevance to the U.S. national interest in promoting central bank independence in South Korea, or in promoting an exclusive focus on inflation.

Just as in this country, the interests of the financial sector are served by anti-inflation policy, which limits growth in the real economy and creates artificially high levels of unemployment.

This shows how financial interests promote a globalist agenda that runs contrary to the U.S. national interest, by disregarding the impact of foreign policy on American industry.

World Financial Markets
The increasing influence of global finance on national economies has progressed with deregulation, publicly financed bailouts, and the explosion of trading in financial markets.

In 2010, world GDP (the productive value generated by all the national economies in the world) was $63 trillion dollars.

In comparison, consider these 2011 value estimates for key financial markets:
- Global bond market - $32 trillion
- Global equity (stock) market - $50 trillion
- Over-the-counter derivatives - $708 trillion
- Foreign exchange (FOREX) market – daily trading volume of $4 trillion

The relative size and explosive growth of these markets is without precedent.

Derivatives are essentially options based on the value of an underlying asset.

The option is derived from the changing value of that asset, hence the name "derivative."

The market value of $708 trillion reflects the face value of the underlying asset, so the magnitude of potential loss is only a fraction of the face value.

Even so, consider a 10 percent loss on these options, equivalent to $70.8 trillion.

The share of that loss incurred by U.S. banks is backed by the federal government.

As part of the financial sector bailout, the federal government agreed to assume this extraordinary level of risk, which had been engineered by Wall Street banks.

The reason the derivatives market is so large, is precisely because it isn't regulated.

The lack of disclosure requirements allows banks to first create these instruments, and then sell them at very high profit margins.

This lack of disclosure was a fundamental cause of the 2008 financial crisis.

Buyers were blind to what the banks paid for the underlying assets that were pooled in derivatives, and had no way of knowing what the margin of profit might be.

While global markets are not regulated, government bailouts of banks have become standard procedure for dealing with financial crises.

The IMF has orchestrated repeated bailouts, which over time have created excess liquidity (too much money) in the system.

It stands to reason that investors should lose money when they make bad decisions.

Banks engaged in excessive lending, or in taking excessive risk of any kind, should be rewarded with destruction of bank capital.

But the Mexican peso crisis of the mid-1990s brought a U.S. commitment of $20 billion, which effectively bailed out the banks involved.

Thereafter, the "too big to fail" philosophy became the world standard, long before the U.S. banking crisis brought the same response in 2008.

Now consider the foreign exchange (FOREX) market. There are a number of participants involved in the FOREX market.

Multinational companies are involved in currency trading, used to hedge against the risk of changing exchange rates.

These companies use multiple currencies to buy and sell goods and services, and to finance payrolls in different countries.

This use of foreign currency by commercial companies accounts for a relatively small percentage of the overall trading volume.

In contrast, speculation has been estimated to account for some 80 to 90 percent of the trading volume.

There is no end use or actual delivery of currency bought by speculators.

Instead, currency is bought on margin and then quickly sold to profit from fluctuations in exchange rates.

Along with banks, there are institutional investors such as pension funds, insurance companies, and mutual funds, as well as hedge funds known for aggressive speculation in the FOREX market.

There is no centralized clearing of FOREX trades, and very little regulation of the cross border transactions that make up the market.

Industry standard leverage is 100 to one, meaning $1 dollar can be used to buy $100 dollars in currency, and then sold on small fluctuations in the exchange rate.

FOREX daily volume was $1.9 trillion in 2004, and increased by more than double to an estimated $4 trillion in 2011.

This incredible volume of trading exceeds the value of U.S. GDP every four days.

The growth of computerized trading with programmed execution of transactions has contributed significantly to this growth in volume.

The relevance here is the massive size of financial markets overall, especially compared to the size of national economies.

Much smaller by comparison are the global bond and equity markets, both of which still dwarf the production value of national economies.

In the 1980s, the bond market was used to finance budget deficits discussed in the twin deficits section above.

As a result, annual sales of U.S. bonds to foreign buyers grew from $50 billion in 1983, to $500 billion in 1993.

Further growth in the value of the bond market, to $32 trillion in 2011, reflects an extraordinary rate of expansion.

Likewise, global stock markets are now valued at $50 trillion, more than 70 percent of world GDP.

New Role of Finance
The massive growth of financial wealth reflects the stunning and unbelievably rapid rise of finance to the position of most powerful actor on the world stage.

Private capital flows to developing countries were over $1 trillion dollars in 2011, which can now be seen in context of the size of world financial markets overall.

Capital flows define the market context in which national governments seek to manage their own economies.

In both the private and the public sector, financial markets dictate priorities.

The market values efficiency as the driving force that maximizes returns.

For private companies, efficiency means cutting wages and benefits to drive up earnings and stock prices.

When too little attention is paid to efficiency, there are huge sums available for hostile takeovers carried out by corporate raiders.

Raiders use borrowed money with tax deductible interest to finance leveraged buyouts, and then sell off or borrow against the assets of the companies they buy.

The downsizing and large scale layoffs that result are irrelevant to computing the financial gains involved.

All that matters for corporate raiders (or for companies trying to defend themselves) is the calculation of efficiency.

This logic of efficiency applies equally to sovereign states, particularly with respect to the market in sovereign bonds.

Efficiency for governments results in lower cost of borrowing and lower interest rates overall.

Countries with budget deficits fear high interest rates that reduce domestic investment, and risk the combined threat of inflation and recession.

For example, the 1987 stock market crash started when Japan began selling U.S. bonds.

Greenspan raised interest rates, which sparked a panic that led to the crash.

Governments strive to ensure a favorable business climate, and to maintain good credit standing in world markets.

This reflects market pressure to reduce deficits without raising taxes, or risk paying higher interest rates to finance the debt.

There is another dysfunctional aspect of financial markets that is important to understand.

This is the phenomena of "crowding in," caused by the combination of a decline in government borrowing, and excess capital in the financial system overall.

When the U.S. budget was in surplus in the late 1990s, the federal government stopped selling new bonds.

This brought enormous flows of foreign investment into the credit market.

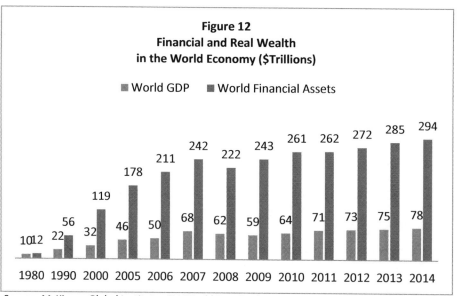

Figure 12
Financial and Real Wealth
in the World Economy ($Trillions)

World GDP World Financial Assets

Source: McKinsey Global Institute, CIA World Fact Book.

Foreign money was invested in dollar denominated debt issued by Fannie Mae and Freddie Mac, and in bonds issued by U.S. corporations.

Foreign investments were also made in the U.S. stock market.

This excess capital was one cause of what Fed chairman Allan Greenspan called "irrational exuberance."

Technology stocks had become highly overvalued, because of an oversupply of credit in the market.

The result was a credit bubble, which after dramatic decline in the NASDAQ, came to be called the dot.com boom.

While countries face pressure to reduce deficits, a decline in government borrowing sets loose an oversupply of capital in the private sector, which serves to create an oversupply of credit.

The way the system operates is dysfunctional, because there is too much money in the market overall.

Figure 12 shows the growth of financial wealth compared to growth in world GDP, from 1980 to 2014.

In 1980 world GDP was $10 trillion, while global financial assets were $12 trillion.

In 2014 world GDP was $78 trillion, while global financial assets had risen to $294 trillion.

The disparity is the result of
- excess profit in both the emerging economies of the developing world and the advanced economies,
- deregulation of capital flows and financial speculation, and
- repeated public sector bailouts of banks and private investors

Excess capital is the reason the real economy only makes up half the global economy.

The other half is artificial, based on low wage labor, excess profits, and speculation.

The unprecedented influence of world financial markets marks the rise of what is clearly a New World Order.

Global markets that control developing countries have just as much power to dictate priorities in Europe and in this country.

The New World Order reflects the power of financial markets to undermine the demand generating process, in every national economy in the world.

Export led growth in developing countries is justified in terms of the necessity of earning foreign exchange to make loan payments.

The result is a collection of national economies that have been restructured, and designed to earn dollars to pay off loans.

These *debt service economies* do nothing to promote the national development of the countries involved.

Instead, consumer markets remain under-developed, and thereby limit the level of demand in the world economy.

Market Globalism
Clearly, the tail is now wagging the dog.

U.S. policy makers promote Wall Street financial interests, at the expense of America's national interest.

American foreign policy drives the unprecedented rise of global finance.

The result has been to establish perpetual dominance of world financial markets over national economies.

Since the mid-1990s, foreign currency devaluations have created an overvalued dollar, making imports less expensive.

In 1994, market reforms in China brought devaluation of the yuan by 34 percent.

Between 1995 and 1996, the Mexican peso was devalued by 70 percent, and by 2006 had lost another 43 percent of its dollar value.

Between 1997 and 2002, nine countries devalued their currencies, including six Asian countries outside China that accounted for the bulk of the U.S. trade deficit.

Devaluations create a flood of cheap imports for American consumers, who in turn have lost their jobs due to offshoring.

The parallel development is the unprecedented growth of world financial markets.

One cause of that growth is clear.

Developing countries have cut spending on programs that promote economic growth, while devoting as much as 50 percent of GDP to debt service.

The relevance for the financial crisis is what Alan Greenspan called a "tsunami of credit" that drove the "irrational exuberance" of the stock market in the late 1990s.

Both offshoring and the buildup of excess liquidity in the system are driven by repeated IMF bailouts of Western banks.

The currency devaluations that follow, not only undermine American manufacturing with cheap imports, but also increase the foreign profits of U.S. multinationals that offshore production.

Offshoring by U.S. multinationals and the rise of global finance are the twin consequences of this process.

The IMF has restructured poor countries as debt service economies, feeding the exponential rise of finance and unregulated speculation.

This is why the financial crisis and the decline of manufacturing are hardly un-related developments.

They are in fact inter-related consequences of mutually reinforcing processes of
- financial deregulation,
- globalization of production, and
- IMF bailouts of Western banks

Many people don't realize they may have lost their job because the dollar is overvalued, relative to other currencies.

It could be the company they used to work for couldn't compete with cheap imports, and went out of business.

Low wage imports and an overvalued dollar make a deadly combination.

Consider where Wall Street's money comes from.

U.S. corporations reported $1.9 trillion in profits in 2011, with 35 percent of the total being foreign profits from operations overseas.

That amounts to more than $650 billion a year in profits from off-shored production.

At the same time, financial assets have been multiplied over and over again through speculation, and have made Wall Street a much more

powerful actor today than it was in the late 1990s.

While the need to change direction is obvious, the underlying problem is Wall Street's political power in Washington.

The extent of that power represents a clear case of ideological capture.

The Wall Street/Treasury Complex
Jagdish Bhagwati coined the term *Wall Street/Treasury complex* to describe
> "a networking of like-minded luminaries among the powerful institutions—Wall Street, the Treasury Department, the State Department, the IMF, and the World Bank," as well as the U.S. Federal Reserve.

In similar fashion, Robert Wade and Frank Veneroso use the term *Wall Street/Treasury/IMF complex* to describe IMF policy as the outcome of Wall Street influence on the U.S. Treasury Department and the Federal Reserve.

Officials at the highest levels of government have adopted Wall Street views on policy, which define the terms of foreign trade and have had devastating impact on the U.S. economy.

Wall Street's influence can be seen in the revolving door between firms like Goldman Sachs and key positions in government.

For example, John Snow, Treasury Secretary during the George H.W. Bush administration, left to become head of Cerberus Capital Management.

Cerberus was a large private equity firm later charged with overseeing management of Chrysler's bankruptcy, during the federal auto bailout of 2008.

Clinton Treasury Secretary Robert Rubin, and George W. Bush Treasury Secretary Hank Paulson were both former heads of Goldman Sachs.

After leaving office, Robert Rubin became chairman of the executive committee for Citigroup.

Federal Reserve chairman Alan Greenspan later became a consultant at Pimco, which is a leading firm in the international bond market.

For decades Wall Street has supplied both the people and the ideology that guides official government policy on management of the economy.

Larry Summers succeeded Robert Rubin as Treasury Secretary in the Clinton administration, and played a key role in lobbying Congress to repeal financial regulations in the late 1990s.

Obama Treasury Secretary Tim Geithner was a former head of the Federal Reserve Bank of New York.

Geithner also served as Under Secretary of the Treasury in the Clinton administration, first under Robert Rubin and later under Rubin's successor, Larry Summers.

Summers and Geithner were architects, with Robert Rubin, of IMF bailouts during the Asian financial crisis.

Those bailouts stipulated economic restructuring (increased exports and reduced government spending) as conditions of IMF assistance.

Bailouts actually deepened the recession in countries receiving IMF loans, and resulted in currency devaluations that brought an explosion of the U.S. trade deficit.

Thereafter, Larry Summers and IMF officials acknowledged that austerity measures were a flawed policy response to the Asian financial crisis.

But the impact of foreign currency devaluation is still with us today.

The process that drives offshoring and destroys American industry is the high dollar policy, orchestrated by officials at the U.S. Treasury.

Wall Street's ideological capture of our government has also been fully bipartisan.

IMF policy during the eight years of the George W. Bush administration was no different than in the eight previous years of the Clinton administration.

In 2008, Larry Summers was appointed director of the White House National Economic Council for the incoming Obama administration.

After widespread criticism of his advocacy of deregulation and support for the financial sector, Summers stepped down in 2010 and became a consultant to a Wall Street hedge fund.

Those who by background were heads of the very firms that profited from unregulated finance and government bailouts, and also served in the Clinton years as architects of the system, later became policy makers in the Obama administration.

IMF policies that promote financial interests led to excessive lending, economic boom and bust, and permanent debt crisis in developing countries.

That same policy orientation has established what is essentially the same cycle in this country.

This remarkable continuity of policy is driven by those at the highest levels of government, who've been promoting the same agenda over a long period.

The Wall Street/Trade Complex
The fundamental cause of U.S. manufacturing decline is the structural disadvantage of American industry in the global system.

America's disadvantage is based on unfair competition with low wage imports, and the undervalued currencies of our trading partners.

The magnitude of disadvantage has progressed in tandem with the unprecedented rise of Wall Street, and the offshoring of production to low wage countries.

International deregulation of finance creates
- boom and bust cycles in poor countries,
- nationalization of debt that bails out private sector banks and speculators,
- devaluation of debtor country currencies,
- dramatic reduction in the cost of foreign labor, and
- excess profits for U.S. multinationals with off-shored production

Offshoring and the rise of Wall Street are twin consequences of financial deregulation and unrestricted trade.

IMF loan programs rely on *unrestricted flows of international capital* and *unrestricted trade* to push export led growth in low wage countries.

Those exports earn the foreign exchange needed to pay off debts to Western banks.

The poor countries involved are caught in a debt trap, in which government support for development is curtailed, both by IMF conditions and by the financial burden of loan payments.

The end result is a pattern of world development that creates too little demand to support markets for American goods.

While U.S. manufacturing declines, and both the trade deficit and the national debt expand, Wall Street has acquired immense wealth through unregulated markets in the world financial system.

Historic trade deficits caused by offshoring, and corresponding record levels of unemployment, are the direct consequence of policies that benefit Wall Street.

The process has brought an unprecedented corruption of our politics.

Elected officials in both political parties embrace policies that undermine America's industrial base and have destroyed the U.S. economy.

America's trade deficit with China, and the corresponding reliance on China to finance our debt, is a system that has been engineered by Wall Street and legitimized by globalist ideology.

The federal government, under both Democratic and Republican administrations, has supported the interests of Wall Street and U.S. companies with offshore production.

This *Wall Street/Trade complex* is in outright collusion with China, to dismantle American industry and replace it with global systems of production.

Mechanism: The goal to maximize shareholder value creates incentive to liquidate American assets and invest in offshore production for higher share prices in the stock market.

Because excess profits from offshoring drive share prices higher, the *Wall Street/Trade complex* benefits from the new terms of engagement between the U.S. and the unregulated global economic system.

At the same time, our politics is corrupted because cheap imports serve the goal of minimizing inflation in the New Economy model of growth.

What policy makers ignore is that globalization of production creates *economic leakage*, which Thomas Palley describes as a *triple hemorrhage for the U.S. economy.*

First, offshoring creates employment leakage: loss of manufacturing means direct job loss that undermines household income in this country.

The second hemorrhage reflects demand leakage, caused by spending on imports.

As household income and credit is used to buy imports, that demand drives growth offshore, outside the U.S. economy.

U.S. consumer debt now remains, *without the jobs that should have been created* by record consumer spending before the onset of recession.

Third, offshoring brings a shift toward foreign investment, and a corresponding loss of investment in this country.

Decline of domestic investment undermines the economy's capacity to create jobs, and robs the country of the industrial base that generates wealth.

The U.S. has suffered an undeniable loss of industrial capacity, as investments in new plant and equipment have shifted from the home market to foreign operations.

Offshoring has forever changed the meaning of trade.

As a result, trade has become *decoupled* from the goal of promoting American exports.

The promotion of unrestricted trade has nothing to do with creating a global market for American goods.

Instead, multinational companies have created global production zones used as export platforms that provide access to low wage labor.

After 1997, offshoring expanded dramatically, as the Asian financial crisis brought currency devaluations throughout the region.

The high dollar serves the interests of Wall Street and U.S. multinationals, while domestic business and American citizens pay the price with high unemployment and stagnation.

The end result is an unconscionable state of affairs, in which Wall Street and U.S. multinationals, in concert with the U.S. Chamber of Commerce, lobby against the economic interests of this country.

Most of us learn the pledge of allegiance in grade school.

The pledge is made to the flag of the United States of America, recited to express our citizenship and commitment to this country.

None of us are citizens of the IMF, the World Bank, or the WTO.

We don't pledge allegiance to Wall Street either.

And Wall Street has no more allegiance to this country than do U.S. multinationals that offshore production to China.

We can insist on policies to lower the trade deficit and reform Wall Street, or we can live with the consequences of letting Wall Street pull the strings in the global economy.

Food for Thought

Wall Street influence in the Treasury Department is matched by a corresponding influence in the IMF and the World Bank.

In the 1990s export booms fueled by international lending in Mexico and then throughout Asia collapsed, followed by debt crisis and IMF bailouts.

Those bailouts of debtor countries were in fact bailouts of Western banks.

The currencies of debtor countries were devalued, while the IMF imposed policies designed to limit consumption and generate trade surpluses needed to earn foreign exchange.

The goal was to restructure debtor country economies to maximize trade surpluses with the U.S., and use the dollars earned to pay back loans.

The impact of IMF policies has been profoundly detrimental to American interests.

The devaluation of debtor country currencies brought the rapid acceleration of offshoring and an explosion of the U.S. trade deficit.

China's currency was devalued in 1994, and is pegged to the dollar.

Following China's entry into the WTO in 2001, the U.S. lost five million jobs in manufacturing, along with nearly three times as many jobs through associated loss in supply chains and re-spending effects.

Meanwhile the doctrine of shareholder value serves to enrich corporate CEOs who close down U.S. plants and move manufacturing overseas.

The loss of American manufacturing is the direct consequence of policies that benefit Wall Street and U.S. multinationals with offshore production—the Wall Street/Trade complex.

Losing the Trade War

Main Points

Currency devaluation lowers the cost of foreign labor, and makes offshoring all the more profitable.

As a result, trade has been transformed by the globalization of production.

Rather than creating a global marketplace for American goods, U.S. multinationals have created global production zones that supply the American market.

At the same time, U.S. policy reflects unilateral, one-way free trade, while other countries practice strategic trade.

Strategic trade views trade as part of a larger policy of strategic development, or promotion of key industries considered critical for economic development.

China represents an extreme case of government sponsorship of industry, and the use of strategic trade as a means to acquire technology and gain control of key resources.

There are also more than 2 million children in China with industrial occupations.

Of those, 1.5 million are under the age of 15 and earn between 40 cents and 60 cents per hour.

American industry faces a structural disadvantage, which reflects the combined impact of subsidies, low wage labor, and the undervalued currencies of our trading partners.

The terms of engagement between the U.S. and the world economy have changed.

Deregulation of finance and the phenomena of the U.S. twin deficits have most clearly evolved to create unintended consequences.

At the same time, trade has been transformed by globalization, which was a new and limited development in the 1980s.

Promotion of free trade for geopolitical reasons seemed entirely reasonable at an earlier juncture in our history.

After World War II, U.S. foreign policy reflected the threat of economic collapse in Europe and the potential rise of socialism.

Providing access to the American market made it possible to rebuild the industrial infrastructure of our post war allies.

Along with the Marshall Plan and other forms of aid, access to the U.S. market was critical to the process of reconstruction in post war Europe, and in Japan during the American occupation.

Thereafter, Taiwan and South Korea also became economic protectorates of the United States, based on access to the American market.

Here again, the use of trade to foster development was consistent in both cases with this country's geopolitical interests at the time.

But after the Soviet empire collapsed in 1989, the rationale for U.S. trade policy began to unravel.

The dysfunctional promotion of export led growth as a tool of Cold War policy now became synonymous with free market ideology.

The historian Ha-Joon Chang conducted a comprehensive study of advanced countries that used tariffs and industrial policy to protect infant industries and foster development.

In addition to Britain and the U.S., the list includes Germany, Sweden, France, Finland, Norway, Belgium, Italy, Austria, Japan, Taiwan, and South Korea.

Chang also found that despite the prevalence of free trade rhetoric in the post war period, the reality in this country and in Europe was not as fully consistent with principles of free trade as is typically portrayed.

In 1962 industrial tariffs ranged from 7 percent to 20 percent in Europe, and averaged 13 percent in this country.

In 1973, the average U.S. industrial tariff was still 12 percent.

Furthermore, spinoffs from U.S. defense and NASA programs were a critical driver of America's lead in advanced technologies.

From the 1950s to the mid-1990s, the federal government provided between 50 and 70 percent of total R&D funding, serving as the unofficial equivalent of industrial policy.

Today most countries engage in strategic planning and support for domestic industry, through some form of industrial policy.

But increasingly since the 1980s, the U.S. has adhered to a "hands off" approach to trade, leaving American manufacturing vulnerable to competition from government supported industry abroad.

Outside the U.S., industrial policy in some form is almost universal.

China represents an extreme case of government sponsorship of industry, and the use of strategic trade as a means to acquire technology and gain control of key resources.

This country has been involved in a trade war with China since the late 1990s, previously described as a war in which only one side is firing the shots.

In 2011 the U.S. had a trade deficit in non-oil goods of $398.8 billion dollars.

The U.S. deficit in non-oil goods with China was $295.4 billion, or 74 percent of the total.

Clearly, China accounts for the overwhelming majority of low wage imports into this country.

U.S. multinationals with supply chains throughout Asia have final assembly completed in China, increasing the overall level of U.S. imports from China.

Multinationals with offshore production are using China as an export platform for goods sold in the American market.

Because of an elaborate system of subsidies, producing in China to sell in the American market is far more profitable than producing in this country for the domestic market.

Consider the advantages to companies using China as an export platform:
- Wages between 80 cents and $1.20 an hour for adult workers
- Chinese currency undervalued by 40 percent, reducing the dollar value of U.S. imports from China by 40 percent
- Child labor – 5.5 million in Asia under age 15 with industrial occupations, which includes 1.5 million in China: Children earn roughly half the wages of adult workers.
- Absence of employee benefits, including payment of overtime.
- Minimal health, safety, or environmental regulations
- Export subsidies between 10 and 20 percent of the exchange value of exports
- China's value added tax (VAT) of 17 percent. Producers receive a 17 percent credit applied to materials bought in China when the finished product is exported.
- The U.S. tax code requires payment of taxes on foreign operations only when profits are brought back to this country.
  Allowing companies to defer taxes encourages additional investment overseas, instead of using profits for domestic investment in this country.

Currency Manipulation
China pegs the yuan to the dollar, at a rate estimated to be undervalued by 40 percent.

Much of the U.S. trade deficit with China is due to this yuan currency peg to the dollar.

The depreciated exchange value of the yuan is equivalent to a subsidy for Chinese exports to America, and a corresponding tariff on U.S. exports to China.

For every dollar in U.S. currency, China can export 40 percent more to America than U.S. companies can export to China.

Floating exchange rates are the key mechanism designed to maintain balanced trade in a free trade system.

If the yuan was allowed to float, a rise in the U.S. trade deficit would cause the dollar to fall in value, relative to the yuan.

The lower dollar would make U.S. goods less expensive, and Chinese goods more costly.

This would bring a rise in U.S. exports to China and a fall in imports from China. The result would be an automatic, or market driven balancing of U.S. - China trade.

This is how floating exchange rates actually work between countries all over the world.

But there is no such thing as free trade without floating exchange rates. The peg of the yuan to the dollar is a fixed exchange rate that rigs the system.

The result is what has become a structural trade deficit with China.

There isn't any way to address China's overwhelming share of the trade deficit, without raising the dollar value of the yuan exchange rate.

But China finances U.S. budget deficits by purchasing Treasury bonds.

As explained in the section on U.S. twin deficits, China's trade surplus is invested in dollar assets in order to reconcile its balance of payments accounts.

The dysfunction inherent in this system is greatly exacerbated by pegging the yuan to the dollar.

The combination of the currency peg and the 40 percent depreciated value of the yuan, accounts for China's overwhelming share of America's trade deficit.

This same combination also accounts for U.S. dependence on China for dollar investments in Treasury bonds, which finance our budget deficit.

The U.S. has run consecutive budget deficits well over a trillion dollars for the last four years.

In 2011 China's holdings of dollar reserves, earned from its trade surplus, were estimated at $2.5 trillion dollars, the largest dollar holdings of any country in the world.

This accumulation of dollar reserves means the U.S. is now dependent on China to a much greater extent than our similar dependence on Japan in the 1980s.

At that time, Japan had the largest reserve of U.S. Treasuries, and initiated the 1987 market crash when it started selling off those bonds.

China's leverage over the U.S. amounts to a form of blackmail, based on the threat of withholding dollar investments in Treasury bonds.

The importance China places on this leverage can be seen in another aspect of the process of how these dollar assets are acquired.

U.S. dollars are initially earned on exports by Chinese producers.

These export companies, including multinational partnerships, are then forced to buy Chinese government bonds denominated in dollars.

The process is called sterilization, and involves a 50 percent subsidy for dollar investments in U.S. Treasury bonds.

Chinese producers are forced to buy government bonds that pay 4 percent interest.

The Chinese government then uses these dollar denominated bonds to buy U.S. Treasuries that pay only 2 percent interest.

This 50 percent difference amounts to hundreds of billions of dollars in subsidies, which China's government provides to make these investments.

Because China is a totalitarian country controlled by the Communist party, there is no political opposition to the cost of these currency subsidies in the annual budget.

Instead, currency subsidies along with a range of other subsidies, are simply mechanisms put in place to achieve China's strategic objectives by rigging its trade relationships with other countries.

This rigged system has been extremely effective in building China's industrial base, financed by exports and matched by the corresponding decline of American manufacturing.

Import/Export controls and dumping
In addition to indirect tariffs on imports from the undervalued yuan, China also imposes direct tariffs of 30 percent on imports.

This combination of indirect and direct tariffs protects domestic industry from foreign competition, and effectively limits exports to the Chinese market.

At the same time, companies in China are provided access to free land, subsidized energy, and essentially unlimited credit at low or zero interest.

Goods producing industries also receive direct subsidies on exports between 10 and 20 percent of the foreign exchange export value.

There are also restrictions on foreign ownership that allow foreign businesses to operate in China only as minority partners of Chinese companies.

Taken together, these controls effectively block foreign access to the domestic market, and serve to protect companies in China from competition.

In addition to these general subsidies and tariffs, there are also quotas and export duties as high as 70 percent on exports of strategic raw materials.

These materials are inputs or key process components essential to heavy industry.

China has also engaged in a directed policy of dumping and predatory pricing used to monopolize the supply of rare earth metals.

Rare earth metals are used in x-ray machines, MRI imaging, PET scans, lasers, magnets, battery electrodes as well as nuclear batteries and electric batteries for hybrid cars, microwave filters, alloy components for computers and aerospace, and high temperature superconductors.

China is now building strategic reserves of these metals used in high technology products.

With only about a third of world reserves, China accounts for more than 90 percent of global production.

This virtual monopoly is the result of long term subsidies and the intentional oversupply of the market, to force down prices below the cost of production and drive competitors out of business.

Control over strategic raw materials and rare metals can also be seen as part of China's growing leverage over developing countries in Asia, Africa, and Latin America.

Chinese banks provided loans equivalent to nearly $1.2 trillion in 2011, including loans for infrastructure projects and development of natural resources throughout the developing world.

The growing debt of developing countries owed to private banks has been described in terms of foreign control of emerging economies.

While borrowing from China has similar implications, the debt incurred is different from debt owed to banks, private investors, or to other countries.

The difference is that China is a totalitarian regime controlled by the Communist party.

Figure 13

American Companies in China

AT&T	Canon Electronics	Eclipse CCTV	HP Computer
Abercrombe & Fitch	Carole Cable	Edge Electronics	Honeywell
Abbott Laboratories	Casio Instrument	Electric Vehicles USA	Hubbell Inc.
Ademco Security	Caterpillar, Inc.	Eli Lilly Company	Huggies
ADI Security	CBC America	Emerson Electric	Hunts-Wesson
AGI- American Gem	CCTV Outlet	Enfamil	ICON Office
AIG Financial	Checker Auto	Estee Lauder	IBM
Agrilink Foods, Inc.	CitiCorp	Eveready	Intel Corp.
Allergan Laboratories	Cisco Systems	Family Dollar Stores	J.C. Penny's
American Eagle	Chiquita Brands	FedEx	J.M. Smucker
American Standard	Claire's Boutique	Fisher Scientific	John Deere
American Tourister	Cobra Electronics	Ford Motors	Johnson Control
Ames Tools	Coby Electronics	Fossil	Johnson & Johnson
Amphenol Corporation	Coca Cola Foods	Frito Lay	Johnstone Supply
Amway Corporation	Colgate-Palmolive	Furniture Brands	JVC Electronics
Analog Devices, Inc.	Colorado Spectrum	GAP Stores	KB Home
Apple Computer	ConAgra Foods	Gateway Computer	Keebler Foods
Armour Meats	Cooper Tire	GE, General Electric	Kenwood Audio
Ashland Chemical	Corning, Inc.	General Foods	Kentucky F. Chickn
Ashley Furniture	Coleman Sp. Goods	General Mills	Kimberly Clark
Associated Grocers	Compaq	General Motors	Knorr Foods
AudioVox	Crabtree & Evelyn	Gentek	K-Mart
AutoZone, Inc.	Cracker Barrel	Gerber Foods	Kohler
Avon	Craftsman Tools	Gillette Company	Kohl's Corp.
Banana Republic	Cummins, Inc.	Goodrich Company	Kraft Foods
Bausch & Lomb, Inc.	Dell Computer	Goodyear Tire	Kragen Auto
Baxter International	Del Monte Foods	Google	Land's End
Bed, Bath & Beyond	Dewalt Tools	Guess?	Lexmark
Belkin Electronics	DHL	Haagen-Dazs	LG Electronics
Best Buy	Dial Corporation	Harley Davidson	Lipton Foods
Best Foods	Diebold, Inc.	Hasbro Company	L.L. Bean, Inc.
Big 5 Sporting Goods	Dillard's, Inc.	Heinz Foods	Logitech
Black & Decker	Dodge-Phelps	Hershey Foods	Libby's Foods
Body Shop	Dole Foods	Hoffman-LaRoche	Linen & Things
Borden Foods	Dollar Tree Stores	Holt's Automotive	Lipo Chemicals
Briggs & Stratton	Dow-Corning	Hormel Foods	Lowe's Hardware
Calrad Electric	Eastman Kodak	Home Depot	Lucent Tech.
Campbell 's Soup	EchoStar	Hoover Vacuum	Lufkin

Source: www.jiesworld.com / accessed 5/6/2015 / based on shipping database, U.S. Customs database, Chinese government publications and database. The companies listed have manufacturing operations in China, and are exporting products from China to the American market. For a list of over 800 American companies in China see http://www.cnn.com/CNN/Programs/lou.dobbs.tonight/popups/exporting.america.

(Figure Continues)

While the economy operates as a capitalist system, that system is controlled by a government with strategic objectives considered far more important than the profits to be made from investments.

The IMF has a long history of providing new loans for countries in crisis, orchestrating bailouts for the banks involved, re-negotiating interest rates and loan repayment schedules, and more recently providing debt forgiveness for highly indebted countries.

China has no such history.

Developing country debt to China is secured by liens on natural resources, typically required on loans for infrastructure to facilitate extraction of those resources.

China holds the mortgage on natural resources throughout the developing world, including oil production and the strategic raw materials and rare metals described above.

China's financial position as the world's banker is financed by its trade surplus with the U.S.

The dollars earned from low wage exports to American consumers are the fundamental source of China's rise as a world power.

At the same time, the U.S. has done virtually nothing in response to China's currency manipulation, or to import tariffs and export subsidies maintained in clear violation of WTO rules.

As a result, the unfair advantage created by these tactics has drawn American companies to offshore production to China.

U.S. multinationals in China benefit from the same export subsidies and low currency values that benefit Chinese companies.

These advantages for U.S. companies in China stand in stark contrast to the lack of government support for industry in this country.

Figure 13 shows a partial listing of U.S. multinationals with export operations in China.

The companies shown reflect both the extraordinary scale of production in China, and the range of U.S. industry involved.

China's growing influence as a creditor for developing countries would not be possible without the unprecedented extent of manufacturing established by U.S. corporate producers in China.

Transfer of Technology
Offshoring of production has severely undermined America's industrial base.

U.S. industry is critical to economic growth, in terms of both employment and the value added in manufacturing.

Figure 13 (Continued)
American Companies in China

Mars Candy	Panvise	Reynolds Alum	Timken Bearing
Martha Stewart	Papa Johns	Revlon	Tommy Hilfiger
Mattel	Payless Shoes	Rohm & Hass Co.	Toro
McCormick Foods	Pelco	Samsonite	Tower Auto
McDonald's	Pep Boy's	Shell Oil	Toy's R Us, Inc.
McKesson Corp.	Pepsico Int.	Schwinn Bike	Trader Joe's
Megellan GPS	PetsMart	Sears-Craftsman	Tripp-lite
Memorex	Petco	Seven-Eleven (7-11)	True Value
Merck & Company	Pfizer, Inc.	Sherwin-Williams	Tupper Ware
Michael's Stores	Phillip Morris	Shure Electronics	Tyson Foods
Mobile Oil	Pier 1 Imports	Shopko Stores	Uniden Elec.
Molex	Pillsbury Co.	Skechers Footwear	Valspar Corp.
Motorola	Pioneer Elec.	SmartHome	Victoria 's Secret
Motts Applesauce	Pitney Bowes	Solar Power, Inc.	Vizio Elec.
Multifoods Corp.	Pizza Hut	Spencer Gifts	Walgreen Co.
Nabisco Foods	Plantronics	Stanley Tools	Walt Disney Co.
National Semicon.	PlaySchool Toys	Staple's	Walmart
Nextar	Polaris Industries	Starbucks Corp.	WD-40 Corp.
Nike	Polaroid	Steelcase, Inc.	Weller Electric
Northrop Grumman	Polo (Ralph Loren)	STP Oil	Western Digital
NuSkin Int.	Post Cereals	Sunkist Growers	Westinghouse
Nutrilite (Amway)	Price-Pfister	SunMaid Raisins	Weyerhaeuser
Nvidia Corp.	Pringles	Sunglass Hut	Whirlpool
Office Depot	Praxair	Sunkist	Wilson Sporting
Olin Corporation	Proctor & Gamble	Subway Sandwiches	Wrigley
Old Navy	PSS World Medical	Switchcraft Elec.	WW Grainger
Olympus Elec.	Pyle Audio	SYSCO Foods	Wyeth Labs
Orion-Knight Elec.	Qualcomm	3-M	Xelite
Pacific Sunwear	Quest One	Target	Xerox
Pamper's	Radio Shack	Tektronix, Inc	Yahoo
Panasonic	Ralph Loren	Texas Instruments	Yum Brands
Pan Pacific Elec.	RCA	Timex	Zale Corp.

Source: www.jiesworld.com / accessed 5/6/2015 / based on shipping database, U.S. Customs database, Chinese government publications and database. The companies listed have manufacturing operations in China, and are exporting products from China to the American market. For a list of over 800 American companies in China see http://www.cnn.com/CNN/Programs/lou.dobbs.tonight/popups/exporting.america.

Offshoring to China fuels that country's acquisition of technology, through transfer of intellectual property and the rights to manufacturing design.

Despite this unprecedented threat, U.S. policy has aided China in its trade war on American industry.

As noted above, there are unfair advantages for U.S. companies that offshore production to China.

But these advantages come at a high price for the companies involved, and also serve to undermine America's capacity for innovation through the transfer of scientific processes and technology.

Foreign companies are required to enter partnerships with Chinese companies, and also have to agree to provide not only technology but also research and development operations to the Chinese partner.

The result has been to transfer not only production, but also the knowledge of manufacturing processes and the design capability for new advancements required to develop more sophisticated products and devices.

The U.S. has lost the ability to produce high technology products in some sectors, and has lost the basis for competitive advantage in others.

For example, computer outsourcing in the late 1980s was limited to contract production of circuit boards.

Over time, what began as limited production led to complete assembly of the finished product in South Korea, Taiwan, or China.

Parent companies then outsourced management of the supply chains involved, and ultimately the design engineering required to create new products.

This transition was a natural outcome of the close relationship between process innovation and product innovation.

When production is outsourced, the associated knowledge and process-engineering expertise tends to follow that production.

Maintaining expertise in the manufacturing process requires ongoing interaction and involvement in production.

This process-engineering expertise is the source of innovation in better process technologies, and is also the source of innovation that creates new and more highly advanced products.

As a result, a growing number of high tech products can no longer be made in this country.

Examples include computers, the Amazon Kindle and other hand held devices, electronic displays and batteries used in cell phones, advanced ceramics, and microchips used in semiconductors.

Figure 14
Child Labor - 2008
(Millions and Percent)

	World (millions)	Percent of World Total	Hazardous Work (millions)	Percent of Age Group
Ages 5 - 11	91	42%	26	29%
Ages 12 - 14	62	29%	27	44%
Total 5 - 14	153	71%	53	36%
Ages 15 - 17	62	29%	62	100%
Totals	215	100%		

	China Mainland (millions)	Hazardous Work (millions)	Regional Totals (millions)	Regional Hazardous (millions)
Ages 5 - 11	14	4	48	14
Ages 12 - 14	10	4	33	14
Total 5 - 14	24	8	81	28
Ages 15 - 17	10	10	33	33
Totals	34	27	114	89

Source: Global Child Labour Developments: Measuring Trends 2004 to 2008, International Programme on the Elimination of Child Labour, International Labor Organization, 2010, tables 5, 6, and 9, pages 7 and 9. World percentages for age groups were applied to total child labor figures provided for Asia & Pacific excluding China, and separately for Mainland China.

The U.S. is also at risk of losing the ability to make a wide range of other products, including carbon composites used for components in aerospace and in wind energy production.

While there is no end to this process of technology transfer in sight, there is also little sign of meaningful change in U.S. policy.

After 30 years of outsourcing, U.S. companies in China finance large scale lobbying campaigns to undermine policy changes that would impact corporate profits.

Even more disturbing is the participation of the American Chamber of Commerce in these efforts.

The interests of U.S. multinationals in China run contrary to the interests of American industry and to the national interests of this country.

While American industry is losing the ability to compete, U.S. multinationals are helping China acquire technology for advanced manufacturing.

Child Labor

Figure 14 shows child labor in the Asia & Pacific region estimated at more than 80 million children under the age of 15, of whom 60 percent are under the age of 12.

These regional totals are important, because multinationals use China as an export platform for supply chain production located throughout Asia.

Precise figures broken down by age group are hard to come by.

The International Labour Organization (ILO) provides world child labor and age group totals, as well as total child labor figures by region.

The percentages shown reflect child labor for the region and the separate breakdown for China reported by the ILO.

Estimates shown for age groups are based on world age group percentages, which were applied to the regional totals reported by the ILO.

The ILO also makes the distinction between children in employment, and the more restricted category of child labor.

For example, the regional total for children in the age 5-14 group engaged in employment was 96 million, of which only 81 million were classified as child labor.

The child labor category excludes children engaged in what is considered permissible light work and those who only work a few hours each week.

Hazardous work by children includes any occupation that has adverse impact on a child's health or safety.

More than a third of children under 15 work in hazardous occupations, such as factory work involving machinery, where small hands are useful in working with equipment.

Child labor in China includes roughly 24 million under the age of 15, of whom 14 million are under the age of 12, with roughly a third of the total engaged in hazardous occupations.

Earning roughly half of adult wages, child workers in China earn between 40 cents and 60 cents an hour.

Seven percent of children in the child labor category have industrial occupations.

That renders a total of 1.5 million children in China, and over 5.5 million in the region as a whole, who are under the age of 15 and have industrial occupations.

As low as wages are for adults, it seems clear that 5.5 million children under age 15, working for 50 cents an hour, have played a significant role in running American manufacturing out of business.

There are yet another 10 million workers in China, and 33 million in the region as a whole, who are between the ages of 15 and 17.

More than 2.3 million in that age group throughout the region have industrial occupations as well.

Beyond the obstacles posed by currency manipulation and strategic trade practiced by many countries including China, the problem for American manufacturing is that it can't compete with child labor.

Food for Thought

The Federal Reserve, the Treasury Department, the IMF and the World Bank have become captive to financial interests.

U.S. Treasury officials were directly involved in orchestrating IMF bailouts that led to 1990s currency devaluations in Mexico and throughout Asia.

Following China's devaluation of the yuan in 1994, Treasury Department officials also lobbied to facilitate China's entry into the WTO.

China's aggressive use of strategic trade amounts to a trade war on American industry.

China uses the devalued yuan in conjunction with a wide range of subsidies and tariffs to create an overwhelming advantage for domestic manufacturing.

That advantage not only benefits domestic Chinese companies, but also U.S. multinationals with offshore production in China.

The result is that U.S. multinationals benefit from China's victory in its trade war on American industry.

With the exception of periodic expressions of outrage in Congress, along with campaign rhetoric that repeats every four years, the U.S. government has been conspicuous in its lack of response.

Turning a blind eye to China's continuous violation of WTO rules is most certainly a policy that originates in the U.S. Treasury Department.

The reason is that China's annual purchase of Treasury bonds is essential to financing the federal budget.

When the U.S. runs a $400 billion trade deficit with China, that deficit is matched by inflows of $400 billion in Chinese capital used to buy Treasury bonds.

China has accumulated over $2 trillion dollars in U.S. Treasuries, more than any other country in the world.

Sadly, China's role as America's banker has created a vacuum in U.S. policy.

The official position of our government is to stand by and do nothing as American industry loses the trade war and our citizens lose their jobs.

Summary

China's policy of strategic trade creates a structural disadvantage for American industry.

Through an elaborate system of import controls and export subsidies, offshoring has been made increasingly profitable for U.S. companies.

Global production has severed the link between trade and the goal of promoting American exports.

Instead, U.S. multinationals have established global production zones in low wage countries that supply the American market.

Because U.S. trade deficits attract foreign capital needed to finance budget deficits, there is limited interest in the impact of offshore production on the American economy.

The U.S. rarely fires a shot in the Trade War with China.

The reason is that China is by far the most important source of foreign capital required for investments in Treasury bonds.

Those investments maintain the system of U.S. debt driven stimulus for consumption.

With rare exceptions, U.S. policy ignores the implications of strategic trade as practiced by China and other countries throughout Asia.

China's WTO violations are hardly relevant. Child labor and the undervalued yuan are irrelevant.

All that matters is that China is the primary source of investment in U.S. Treasuries, without which the system of debt driven growth would collapse.

Trade deficits bring foreign capital into the country used to finance budget deficits.

At the same time, foreign investment supports the credit fueled booms and asset price inflation that define the model of growth we call the New Economy.

What I call the *Wall Street/Trade complex* is that collection of interests that benefit from the New Economy at the expense of real economic growth, national economic development, and national sovereignty.

The New Economy is in fact the domestic consequence of *Market Globalism*, in which U.S. policy promotes unrestricted flows of international capital and unrestricted trade with low wage countries.

Offshoring of manufacturing, record trade deficits and the wholesale deindustrialization of America are the result.

Support for unrestricted finance and unrestricted trade marks a sea change in American politics, which became fully bipartisan after the 1992 election.

For example, the Clinton administration gang of four, Robert Rubin, Larry Summers, Tim Geithner, and Alan Greenspan
- lobbied for financial deregulation that included repeal of Glass-Steagal,
- succeeded in getting legislation passed that prevented regulation of derivatives, and
- orchestrated the IMF's use of currency devaluation and export led growth to pay off poor country debt to Western banks.

Historic loss of American manufacturing caused by currency devaluations abroad, and the loss of associated employment in this country were not relevant to the logic of such policy.

Instead, all that mattered was protecting the interests of Wall Street and U.S. multinationals that define the *Wall Street/Trade complex*.

Government today represents Wall Street and U.S. multinationals with offshore production, while showing complete disregard for the fundamentals of the American economy.

The public welfare and the national interest are secondary considerations, because campaign finance laws guarantee political influence through corporate contributions that are no longer limited.

John McArthur (editor of Harper's magazine) in a recent interview was asked about the Trans-Pacific trade deal being promoted by president Obama.

His answer was phrased in terms of Wall Street's influence in Washington:

> "Wall Street loves free trade because it equals cheap labor. All these trade agreements…are investment agreements that make it safer for American corporations to set up shop in cheap labor locales.
>
> Wall Street thinks that's great. It's great for the shareholders and it's great for the corporations —the profits go up.
>
> So as long as the cash keeps coming to both (political) parties, from those interested parties, …short of a revolution….short of an uprising…you're not going to see any change."

The remainder of the interview centered on the corrupting influence of Wall Street money in politics.

McArthur described both the Clinton and Obama administrations as alliances between Wall Street, business supporters of NAFTA, and the Democratic party.

Obama's former chief of staff, Romm Emmanuel, and his successor Bill Daley, were known as chief lobbyists for passage of NAFTA during the Clinton administration.

Despite campaign rhetoric to the contrary, Obama has done nothing to mitigate the loss of nearly a million manufacturing jobs from NAFTA.

Instead, the president has promoted a new trade deal with Asia known as "NAFTA for the Pacific."

McArthur also described potential Democratic nominees as being intimidated by Hillary Clinton because of the vast amounts of money she is expected to raise in the 2016 election.

The corrupting influence of money in politics is not lost on Republican senator John McCain, who is well known as the co-sponsor of the McCain-Feingold campaign finance reform bill.

McCain described the 2010 Supreme Court ruling in *Citizens United*, which led to formation of super PACs, as "one of the worst decisions I have ever seen."

The *Citizens United* ruling allows corporations to make unlimited campaign contributions, on the basis of free speech and the legal status of corporations being equivalent to the status of people with individual rights.

The *Wall Street/Trade complex* has made trillions of dollars dismantling American industry, setting up shop overseas, and using slave labor to make goods that are shipped to the U.S. market

Now the *Citizens United* ruling makes it legal for that same complex of interests to make unlimited and undisclosed contributions to political campaigns.

The corrupting influence of money in politics is fully bipartisan, as Republicans and Democrats alike turn their backs on small business and what remains of American companies that still have domestic production.

Serving the interests of the *Wall Street/Trade complex* takes priority, because that's where the money comes from to fund political campaigns.

Voting has been reduced to a choice between Corn Flakes and Rice Krispies—behind the difference in the labels, the underlying brand is the same.

For the majority of candidates, a vote for someone running for the House of Representatives, or the Senate, or for president, no matter the party, is a vote for the *Wall Street/Trade complex*—Wall Street banks and U.S. multinationals with offshore production.

This is the political reality that has run the American economy into the ground.

End Game

China's pursuit of strategic trade includes currency manipulation and a wide range of incentives and subsidies that encourage offshoring of U.S. manufacturing.

After China's entry into the WTO, this country lost nearly 5 million jobs in manufacturing.

At the same time, domestic investment has declined, while U.S. corporate profits from foreign operations are now four times the level of the 1960s.

Low wage imports have undermined American wages and the demand generating process in the U.S. economy.

The New Economy model of debt driven growth based on low wage imports and asset price inflation is now bankrupt.

Households are now far less able to take on more debt, so that continued debt driven consumption is no longer a viable source of growth.

Today the U.S. economy is on life support, relying on stimulus both from deficit spending and expansion of the money supply carried out by the Federal Reserve.

The Fed bought toxic mortgages from Wall Street banks at the rate of $75 billion a month in 2013, and then at $40 billion a month in 2014, along with absorbing U.S. debt by purchasing Treasury notes.

Yet all we hear is how we should cut spending to balance the budget, while the Federal Reserve prints money out of thin air to the tune of another $1.5 trillion to continue bailing out the banks.

Implementing a policy of austerity would be catastrophic, because the economy would collapse without an adequate level of spending.

Even so, the administration seems almost equally deluded as to what will be required to restore the growth of demand and output to levels adequate for the economy to generate significant gains in employment.

Stimulus now has limited impact, because spending on imports leaks out of the economy.

Stimulating demand for imports does nothing to reduce employment, and will only perpetuate stagnation and risk further loss of productive capacity that results from offshoring.

The administration and the Federal Reserve are engaged in a continuing effort to maintain demand through stimulus in the hopes of restoring consumption.

As necessary as that policy is as an interim measure, it also represents abject failure to address the demand generating process in the economy.

This country now faces a mandate for survival.

Industrial policy that includes large scale strategic investment will be required.

Investment adequate to build a manufacturing base in high value-added industries that can re-establish an industrial base will be required to create wealth and jobs.

Advanced technology investments made by the administration between 2009 and 2012 are to be applauded.

Those investments were an intelligent use of stimulus, designed to promote industry rather than consumption.

But the reality is the level of investment required is far greater than what is reflected in administration proposals.

Political opposition notwithstanding, strategic investment offers the only hope to restore the country's industrial base and establish a foundation for permanent recovery.

Deindustrialization

Main Points

In the late 1970s and early 1980s, high interest rates brought recession and a highly overvalued position for the dollar.

Between 1979 and 1992, employment in manufacturing declined by four million jobs.

While the dollar was later devalued in 1985/1986, it was not until 1991 that the trade deficit was brought into balance.

The years between 1992 and 1997 were a period of dollar stability, which brought stability to U.S. manufacturing as well.

Thereafter, currency devaluation in Mexico and throughout Asia returned the dollar to a highly overvalued position.

Between 1998 and 2010, manufacturing employment fell by six million jobs.

But the impact on the economy has been far greater than direct job loss in manufacturing.

Between 1998 and 2010, the loss of six million jobs in manufacturing also brought additional loss of
- more than 10 million supply chain jobs, and
- 7 million jobs caused by the lost impact of re-spending

Between 1960 and 1984, net non-residential fixed investment averaged 4 percent per year.

Compared to that historic average, domestic investment since the mid-1980s has declined by $4 trillion dollars.

In the same period, total foreign investment by U.S. corporations amounted to a corresponding figure of $4.9 trillion dollars.

High interest rates were initiated in 1979 as anti-inflation policy under Fed chairman Paul Volcker.

Manufacturing employment declined by 2.1 million jobs between 1979 and 1982, and by another 1.9 million between 1982 and 1992.

While the dollar was devalued between 1985 and 1987, the trade deficit was not brought back into balance until 1991.

Between 1992 and 1997 there was minimal loss of industry, corresponding to the period of dollar stability.

Figure 15
Impact of Manufacturing Job Loss
1998 - 2010 (millions of jobs)

Direct Manufacturing Jobs Lost	Supply Chain Employment	Re-spending Employment
6.0	10.0	7.0

Direct Job Loss:	6.0
Supply Chain Job Loss:	10.0
Re-spending Job Loss:	7.0
Total Loss of Employment:	23.0

Source: Josh Bivens, 2003. Updated Employment Multipliers for the U.S. Economy. (Washington, D.C.: Economic Policy Institute). No. 268, Table 8.

Figure 16
Alternative Measures of Unemployment

		July 2012 *Percent	Jul-12 Unemployed (Millions)	July 2015 *Percent	Jul-15 Unemployed (Millions)
U-1	Persons unemployed 15 weeks or longer, as a percentage of the civilian labor force	4.3%	6.7	2.0%	3.1
U-2	Job losers and persons who completed temporary jobs, as a percentage of the civilian labor force	4.6%	7.1	2.7%	4.2
U-3	Total unemployed, as a percentage of the civilian labor force (official unemployment rate)	8.6%	13.3	5.6%	8.8
U-4	U-3 plus discouraged workers, as a percentage of the civilian labor force plus discouraged workers	9.1%	14.1	6.0%	9.4
U-5	U-4 plus all other marginally attached workers, as a % of the civilian labor force plus all marginally attached	10.0%	15.5	6.7%	10.5
U-6	U-5 plus total employed part-time because full time jobs are not available	15.1%	23.4	10.8%	17.0

Source: Bureau of Labor Statistics. Persons marginally attached to the labor force are those who currently are neither working nor looking for work but indicate that they want and are available for a job and have looked for work in the past 12 months. Discouraged workers, a subset of the marginally attached, have given a job-market related reason for not currently looking for work. Persons employed part time for economic reasons are those who want and are available for full-time work but have had to settle for a part-time schedule. Figures reflect un-adjusted rates.

But after the mid-1990s, currency devaluations in Asia and Latin America returned the dollar to a highly overvalued position.

The impact was to make imports far cheaper and drive the trade deficit to unprecedented levels.

Today there isn't any way American manufacturing can compete with the advantages of producing in China.

The impact since China was admitted to the WTO in 2001 has been devastating.

From 1998 through 2001 manufacturing lost over 1.1 million jobs.

From 2002 through 2010, manufacturing lost another 4.9 million jobs, for total loss since 1998 of 6 million jobs.

Figure 15 shows the cumulative loss of manufacturing jobs between 1998 and 2010.

The decline is especially troubling because those jobs have been lost in the most productive sector of the economy.

Due to extensive product supply and distribution channels, secondary jobs are also created in support of manufacturing, called supply chain jobs.

When employees spend their paychecks, that spending also has ripple effects that support even more jobs in other areas of the economy.

Those indirect employment effects add up to a loss of more than 17 million jobs, above and beyond the loss of 6 million jobs reflecting direct employment in manufacturing.

The combined total impact comes to a loss of more than 23 million jobs between 1998 and 2010.

While it's easy enough to say the loss of manufacturing employment has been offset by job gains in other sectors, recent levels of unemployment don't support that argument.

Figure 16 shows alternative measures of unemployment.

There has been extensive criticism of the official U-3 rate as generating dramatic under-reporting of the actual level of unemployment.

For example, the official unemployment rate doesn't count marginally attached workers (temporary and short term employees) or those who only have part-time jobs.

Adding marginally attached workers and those forced to take part-time jobs to the official U-3 rate renders the U-6 rate, which in August 2012 was 15.1 percent – more than 23 million people unemployed.

U-6 data showing over 23 million people unemployed was cited by Republican candidate Mitt Romney in the run up to the 2012 election.

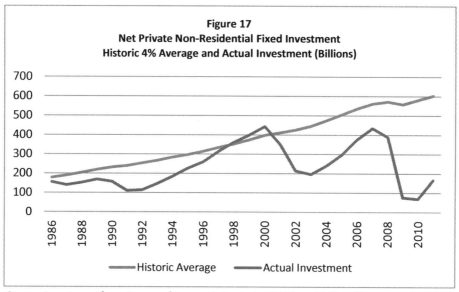

Source: Investment from Bureau of Economic Analysis; GDP from National Income and Product Accounts.

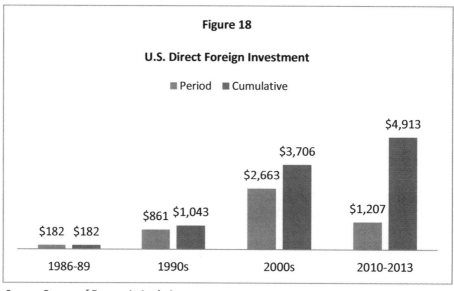

Source: Bureau of Economic Analysis

In 2015, despite the lower levels of unemployment shown, labor force participation reached the lowest level on record.

When working age people stop looking for work and drop out of the labor force altogether, the labor force participation rate goes down.

If labor force participation was the same as in 2008, there would be another 5.5 million people counted in the unemployment figures for 2015.

That change would bring the U-6 figure back to nearly 23 million people unemployed in 2015.

The number of people on food stamps reached an all-time high in 2013, and was still more than 45 million people in 2015.

This country's manufacturing base has been sent overseas, and the employment generated by that production has been lost.

In 2013 there were 5 million fewer jobs in manufacturing than in 1997, while in the same period manufacturing output declined by 35 percent.

The trade deficit and job loss in manufacturing are two sides of the same coin.

Between 1998 and 2010 this country imported $7.3 trillion more in goods than it exported, with corresponding loss of 6 million jobs in manufacturing.

This extraordinary transformation has been matched by a corresponding rise of U.S. corporate profits outside this country and a corresponding fall in productive investment in the domestic economy.

Between 1960 and 1984, net non-residential fixed investment averaged 4 percent per year.

Figure 17 shows the difference between the historic average and actual investment, called the investment gap.

The *cumulative* loss of domestic investment represented by that gap comes to $4 trillion dollars since the mid-1980s.

In 2013 net private non-residential fixed investment was less than 2 percent of GDP, with an investment gap over $338 billion dollars.

At the same time, while domestic investment has declined, U.S. foreign investment has been rising.

Figure 18 shows U.S. direct foreign investment.

In 2013 the investment gap for the U.S. economy was $338 billion, while U.S. foreign investment was $311 billion.

Since the mid-1980s, the *cumulative* loss of investment for the U.S. economy was $4 trillion, while the *cumulative* total for foreign investment was $4.9 trillion.

Not surprisingly, there is a very close match between the two sets of figures.

Domestically we see the negative feedback cycle of excess profits leading to lower demand, lower investment, and then to further decline in demand.

Since the 1980s slow and distorted growth has generated trillions of fewer dollars in production than would have been realized at the historic average rate of growth.

Today the wage share of productivity is less than half what it was in 1973, and *annual* wages from employment are $1.3 trillion less than they would be if the proportion of wage income in the economy was at pre-1974 levels.

Now without question the economy lacks the level of demand required to justify the investment we need for recovery.

Yet corporations have some $2 trillion dollars in cash that isn't being invested.

Those productive investments aren't made when there isn't enough demand in the economy.

In the aftermath of the financial crisis, more than $7.8 trillion was provided by the Federal Reserve to prevent the collapse of the banking system.

Yet even today the banks continue to hoard cash, and corporations are still not making the productive investments essential to job growth and economic recovery.

Food for Thought

Since the mid-1990s, foreign currency devaluations have created an overvalued dollar, making imports less expensive.

As a result, between 1998 and 2010 the U.S. lost
- 6 million jobs in manufacturing,
- 10 million jobs in supply chains, and
- 7 million jobs that would otherwise have been supported through re-spending

The total loss of more than 23 million jobs is supported by official statics on unemployment.

In August 2012, the Labor Department's U-6 estimate of 23 million people out of work was quoted by Mitt Romney in the campaign for the 2012 election.

Another clear relationship is that between the investment gap in the U.S. economy, compared to U.S. foreign investment overseas.

Between 1960 and 1984, net business investment averaged 4 percent per year.

Thereafter, net business investment declined, to an average of 2.7 percent since 1986, and only 2.1 percent since 2004.

The investment gap is the difference between actual business investment and what would have been invested if the historic average of 4 percent had been maintained.

From 1986 to 2014 the investment gap totaled more than $4 trillion dollars.

In the same period, the cumulative value of U.S. foreign investment was $4.9 trillion dollars.

Since the mid-1980s, business investment in this country has declined by nearly 50 percent.

In the same period, investment has been shifted to low wage countries overseas.

Main Points

Since the 1980s, the New Economy has been described as a post industrial economy, based on new technologies and an increasing reliance on services to generate growth.

In manufacturing, economies of scale that drive productivity bring higher wages than in other sectors.

Weekly wages in manufacturing are 20 percent higher than in service sector occupations.

Manufacturing also creates jobs in the service sector.

For example, every million jobs in manufacturing create an additional 580,000 jobs in service sector occupations.

The use of computers throughout the economy has also blurred the distinction between manufacturing and services.

Manufacturing and virtually every economic sector are now heavily dependent on information technology and the continuous evolution of computer software.

Finally, offshoring that has undermined manufacturing poses an even greater threat to jobs in the service sector.

Virtually any job function integrated with computer systems is at risk.

Between 30 million and 40 million jobs are potentially subject to offshoring, from computer programing to design for manufacturing and advertising, to accounting and paralegal services.

Despite the inherent and unprecedented threat posed by offshoring, economists and high ranking officials continue to promote unrestricted trade.

The idea is that the declining share of the U.S. economy accounted for by manufacturing demonstrates the relatively greater importance of services.

In fact, the transition away from manufacturing has been accompanied by slow economic growth and high real rates of unemployment.

The Myth of the Service Economy

A 1983 cover article in Time Magazine described this country's transition from a focus on heavy industry to a New Economy based on newly emerging technologies.

Since then the alternate label in common usage refers to the Service Economy as the basis for a post-industrial society.

Just as globalization has been presented as inevitable, the shift to services has been presented as a natural transition, no different than the transition from agrarian to industrial society at an earlier stage of development.

This argument doesn't hold water for a number of important reasons.

Returns from economies of scale that predominate in manufacturing generate much higher productivity than in other economic sectors.

Manufacturing jobs also pay higher wages, with weekly wages averaging 20 percent higher than for service sector jobs.

The distinction between manufacturing and service sector occupations has also become increasingly blurred.

Design, manufacturing, marketing, sales, finance, and back office accounting and other operations are all heavily dependent on information technology and new developments in computer software.

Advanced manufacturing relies on computer-controlled equipment and focuses on innovative industries like semiconductors, computers, advanced medical devices, clean energy technologies, pharmaceuticals, and applications in nanotechnology.

The complexity of modern manufacturing requires interaction among a wide variety of experts from different disciplines.

Development of new products is also critically dependent on process innovations associated with geographic clustering of related manufacturing, supply chain, research, and educational facilities.

Geographic clustering often results in co-location of R&D activities that drive innovation in manufacturing and are also essential to innovation in the service sector.

For example, new internet services, telecommunications, computer systems design, and scientific research are often spin-offs of industry-funded R&D.

The manufacturing sector accounts for two thirds of private sector R&D and employs 64 percent of the nation's scientists and engineers.

As with innovation in industry, the continuing development of high tech services requires interaction with the pool of skilled researchers who create technologically advanced hardware and software.

Extensive backward and forward linkages through supply chains also create significant impact from manufacturing on service sector employment.

Data provided by the Manufacturing Institute show the impact of manufacturing on other sectors through an employment multiplier of 1.58 jobs.

That means every million jobs in manufacturing supports an additional 580,000 jobs in sectors outside manufacturing.

These linkages also work in reverse, so that decline in manufacturing has led to a corresponding decline in the economy overall.

Between 2001 and 2008 employment decline in manufacturing was over 28 percent, while the average decline in service sector occupations was nearly 16 percent.

At the same time, offshoring may have even greater impact on service sector jobs than on employment in manufacturing.

Studies by Princeton economist Alan Blinder and others have shown that some 25 percent of all jobs could be subject to offshoring.

Many jobs in the service sector are much more vulnerable to offshoring than jobs in manufacturing.

With the development of the internet, job functions involved in call centers, computer programming, reading medical data such as X-rays and MRIs, medical transcription, income tax preparation, and title searching are being off-shored.

According to Blinder, who served on the Council of Economic Advisors in the Clinton administration, between 30 million and 40 million jobs in this country are vulnerable to offshoring.

Food for Thought

The first myth of the Service Economy is that the loss of manufacturing reflects a natural transition to an economy driven by Services.

Between 1998 and 2011, productivity growth of 3.3 percent in manufacturing (not including computers) was more than twice the rate of 1.5 percent for Services.

This is consistent with the historic role played by manufacturing as the fundamental driver of economic development.

It is manufacturing, more than any other sector that drives productivity, while productivity is the basis for rising standards of living.

Manufacturing also has by far the largest employment multiplier — 3 jobs in manufacturing support another 5 jobs in supply chains.

The second myth of the Service Economy is generated by the fact that offshoring is almost always discussed in terms of manufacturing.

In fact, Service sector occupations are even more susceptible to offshoring than are jobs in manufacturing.

With advances in telecommunications and internet applications, virtually any job involving research, design, customer service or technical support services can be outsourced.

Alan Blinder estimates some 25 percent of all jobs—between 30 million and 40 million, are susceptible to offshoring.

What matters about the mythology of a post-industrial society driven by a New Service Economy is that it serves as a cover story for those who profit from offshoring—Wall Street and U.S. multinationals with offshore production.

The Circle of Destruction

Main Points

The precursor to the 1970s stagnation was reaching the limits of world demand in the late 1960s.

In the 1970s, rising oil prices raised the cost of manufactured goods, further undermining demand for American exports.

The reaction was deregulation of industry, which was intended to reduce the cost of labor.

The impact was
- stagnant wages domestically, and
- investment leakage through offshoring

As spending on imports increased,
- unemployment rose, and
- domestic investment declined

At the same time, as the trade deficit grew, inflows of foreign capital increased, and drove up stock and house prices.

The result was that stagnation in the real economy was offset by expansion of the financial economy.

This process drives the circle of destruction, with demand and investment leakage driving ever greater spending on imports.

The result is stagnation in wages, which define the level of demand needed to attract investment in the U.S. economy.

As we've seen, the terms of engagement between the U.S. and the world economy have been transformed.

We can now construct a bird's eye view that illustrates the process and serves to highlight the problems policy needs to address.

As previously shown in the circle of stagnation, underinvestment in production generates excess profits that lead to speculation and stagnant demand in a continuous negative feedback cycle.

But now the context of the global economy has added another dimension to the process of stagnation, which is economic leakage with regard to both investment and demand.

Figure 19
The Circle of Destruction

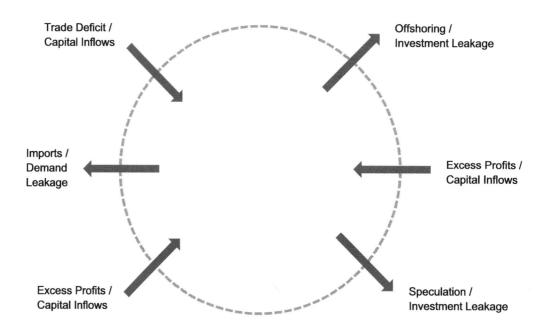

Leakage in Investment and Demand

1) The initial cause of the 1970s stagnation was that production exceeded the level of world demand. The lack of consumer markets throughout the developing world set limits on demand that disrupted the circle of growth.

   While those limits were reached in the late 1960s, the oil price rise of the 1970s raised the cost of manufactured products, further undermining demand.

2) Second, the reaction was to seek ways to reduce costs through deregulation, which reduced labor costs.

   This brought down-sizing and lower wages and benefits domestically, as well as investment leakage through offshoring to foreign countries in search of low wage labor.

3) Third, imports of consumer items generate what is called a leakage of demand. Every dollar spent on imports is a dollar not spent in the domestic economy.

   The U.S. trade deficit reflects an excessive reliance on imports, disrupting the circle of growth by reducing demand, and also creating disincentives for domestic investment.

The impact can be seen in the growth of U.S. corporate profits from foreign operations, from 6 percent of total profits in the 1960s, to an average since 2008 of 22 percent.

At the same time, domestic investment as a percentage of GDP declined, from 4 percent in the 20 years before 1984, to an average 2.7 percent since 1986, and only 2.1 percent since 2004.

Thus, demand leakage from imports and investment leakage are two sides of the same coin.

Offshoring of production reduces domestic investment, and also creates the supply of imports that undermine domestic demand.

The magnitude of investment leakage represents an unanticipated shift away from domestic investment.

In the previous discussion of stagnation, the shift from *productive* investment to financial speculation was shown to undermine the demand generating process in the economy.

That process is made worse by investment leakage, created by offshoring (manufacturing and services) to low wage countries.

Likewise, demand leakage from imports further undermines the demand generating process.

The reason is that stagnant wages in this country (caused in part by spending on imports), undermine demand even further, creating a downward spiral.

At the same time, the twin deficits mechanism brings inflows of foreign capital that are the mirror image of the trade deficit.

Every country's balance of payments must balance.

For the U.S. that means a $500 billion trade deficit drives a corresponding $500 billion in foreign capital flowing into the country.

So while the trade deficit creates demand leakage and stagnation in the real economy, it also brings inflows of foreign capital that drive asset price inflation and artificially expand the financial economy.

The value of demand leakage from the trade deficit is equal to the value of capital inflows.

This explains how credit bubbles make the economy appear stable and growing.

In the aggregate, stagnation in the real economy is offset by asset price inflation and expansion of the financial economy.

This combination drives the New Economy, with asset price inflation overshadowing stagnation in demand and production in the real economy.

What we need is to stimulate demand for things that are made in this country.

But thanks to policies that expand the trade deficit, our ability to stimulate *domestic demand* for *domestic production* is now limited.

Elements of those same policies have also limited the development of consumer markets abroad, making the effort to increase U.S. exports a lost cause.

Clearly, capital inflows that serve to expand the financial economy have also served to obscure the extent of stagnation in the productive economy.

That's why the economy is actually in much worse shape than it might seem, with the threat of price deflation being far greater than most people realize.

What is sheer lunacy is that the illusion of growth has been maintained by taking on long term debt and selling U.S. assets to finance consumption.

No one would consider running for office on that kind of platform, because they wouldn't get elected.

This perverse outcome results from the mechanism of the twin deficits, which makes it possible for the federal government to run budget deficits without raising taxes.

Food for Thought

In the circle of stagnation, higher productivity no longer has the effect of raising wages.

Instead, underinvestment in production generates excess profits that lead to speculation and stagnant demand in a continuous negative feedback cycle.

Offshoring and trade deficits exacerbate the problem, by creating investment leakage, employment leakage, and demand leakage.

This country is trapped in a circle of destruction, in which
- offshoring moves investment offshore,
- offshoring moves employment offshore, and
- domestic demand is undermined by spending on imports

Now the dysfunction of the circle of stagnation has been amplified exponentially, due to multiple forces that limit demand for domestic production.

In parallel with Krugman's use of the term "Depression Economics," policies that might otherwise raise demand don't work, because raising demand no longer means raising demand for domestic production.

Instead, higher demand now translates into higher spending on imports, so that the problem of too little demand for domestic production seems impossible to solve.

Main Points

In the mid-1990s foreign currency devaluations created a flood of cheap imports, as well as a surge of foreign capital entering the U.S. credit market.

The impact was two-fold.

Between 1998 and 2010, employment in American manufacturing declined by 6 million jobs.

As we've seen, direct job loss in manufacturing was accompanied by additional job loss in supply chains and from lost impact of re-spending, totaling more than 17 million jobs.

While offshoring brought the loss of 23 million jobs, the trade deficit brought corresponding inflows of foreign capital.

Between 1997 and 2007, expansion of the U.S. credit market included nearly $4 trillion of foreign capital.

This created an over-supply of credit, and drove up stock and house prices.

In 2008, economic growth based on debt-driven consumption collapsed.

The economy that remains is now crippled, because it has been stripped of productive capacity through offshoring.

In combination, deficit spending and intervention by the Federal Reserve have prevented collapse and a return of Depression era deflation.

This stimulus has been critical as an interim measure, because the economy would collapse without it.

What must be acknowledged is the annual investment deficit of roughly $300 billion dollars.

For private sector investment to reach the 1964 – 1982 average (4% of GDP), domestic investment would have to increase by $300 billion a year.

The only way to achieve that objective is for government to provide a substantial portion of the investment required.

SWIFT Act proposals call for public investment of $300 billion a year, to offset the annual investment deficit of $300 billion in the private sector.

Policy makers no longer have the option of simply providing stimulus for consumption.

Instead, the economy's capacity to generate wealth and jobs will have to be restored.

The Lender of Last Resort

Between 1982 and 2008 the U.S. imported $7.4 trillion more in goods and services than it exported.

As a result, $7.4 trillion entered the country through financial inflows that drove up asset prices and were used to finance budget deficits.

This unprecedented amount of money flowing into the country created artificial growth throughout the economy, culminating in the stock market boom of the 1990s and the housing boom that developed near the end of the decade.

In the mid-1990s austerity programs forced upon debtor countries by the IMF led to currency devaluations that exacerbated both the trade deficit and the corresponding inflows of foreign capital.

In the process, the structure of the U.S. economy was transformed.

While manufacturing lost over eight million jobs, rising stock and housing prices created the wealth that led to an economy dominated more by services than production.

But this model of growth depends on consumption tied to ever-increasing debt.

When the limits of consumer debt were reached in 2008, the model collapsed and the financial sector collapsed along with it.

Today the U.S. economy is crippled, and is being propped up by continued stimulus from government spending and intervention by the Federal Reserve to sustain it.

Yet the Fed is also confronted with a dilemma, because over time it has lost control over credit creation.

The first sign the Fed was losing control came in the late 1990s.

In 1998 Russia's debt crisis and subsequent default led to the collapse of Wall Street hedge fund Long Term Capital Management (LTCM), which was heavily invested in the Russian bond market.

The collapse of LTCM triggered a crisis similar to that of 2008, in that losses and the exposure of other firms throughout the financial sector were of such scale as to threaten collapse of the entire system.

Ultimately the Fed organized a bailout in which 14 firms bought 90 percent of LTCM for $3.625 billion dollars.

While the bailout saved the system from collapse, the Fed also lowered interest rates three times in three months in the fall of 1998, essentially as a means of reassuring the markets.

In the context of strong economic growth at the time, the Fed's move to lower rates was exactly the opposite of policy consistent with basic principles of economy policy.

With money flowing into the country because of the trade deficit, the Fed's move accelerated the run up in stock prices and also drove the start of the housing boom.

This was the first time the trade deficit was shown to be destabilizing, because it created inflows of capital and excess credit that interfered with the Fed's ability to manage the economy.

At a time when the Fed should have raised rates to slow down the boom, rates were instead lowered to alleviate concerns on Wall Street.

Subsequently, the dot.com bubble burst and brought the 2002 collapse of the NASDAQ exchange on which tech stocks were traded.

The Fed lowered rates from 6.5 percent in 2000 to 1 percent by August 2003, and successfully mitigated what might otherwise have been a severe recession.

But then between 2004 and 2006 the Fed raised rates to 5.25 percent on federal funds it loans to banks, in an effort to slow the boom in the housing market.

While this had long been the method of controlling interest rates, there was very little change in the mortgage rates the Fed was trying to raise.

The availability of money in the system had by then become such that the Fed's increase in the funds rate had limited impact on the credit markets.

The excess liquidity created by the trade deficit has essentially overwhelmed the system.

In the aftermath of the financial crisis, rates were lowered to 2 percent in 2008, and then to 0.25 percent in 2009 and kept near zero through late-2015.

Worse still, in tandem with the financial sector bailout the Fed also bought $2.3 trillion in bonds, which it calls "off-balance sheet" reserves.

The Fed then made that money available for banks to borrow, thereby expanding the money supply as a way to encourage lending.

Unfortunately, these measures have had limited impact.

Businesses and consumers continue to have difficulty qualifying for loans, because banks are sitting on reserves to shore up their balance sheets instead of lending.

While the Fed had contemplated "quantitative easing," to further increase the money supply, chairman Bernanke before leaving office also expressed concern about the potential risk of inflation.

Former Fed chairman Paul Volcker has also warned of potential inflation, and appears to some to be re-living his war against inflation in the 1970s.

A well-known lesson of history is that generals tend to fight the last war.

The economic environment today bears no resemblance to the high inflation of the 1970s.

Policy makers need to recognize the current extent of stagnation as a potential path to deflation.

Alan Greenspan acknowledged the threat of deflation in 2003 after the dot.com crash when interest rates were drastically cut to 1 percent to avoid recession.

Deflation remains the issue today, because the private sector is continually deleveraging from the high prices of the real estate boom that led to the crisis.

Most recently, economic growth in 2015 was reported at just 2 percent, while the rate of inflation is zero.

Policy makers also need to recognize that economic stimulus for consumption, while necessary as an interim measure, will simply perpetuate the failed model of debt-based consumption as the engine of growth.

An essential aspect of the debt-fueled growth model is government stimulus to spur growth, by keeping interest rates low and increasing the money supply.

This amounts to financial engineering carried out by the Federal Reserve to perpetuate nominal growth, or growth at face value, without regard to requirements of real growth.

The requirement for real growth is expansion of production in the real economy.

Continued reliance on stimulus is equivalent to doing nothing to address the demand generating process in the economy, which guarantees a catastrophic outcome that could unfold sooner than we think.

The Federal Reserve is the lender of last resort, committed to financial sector bailouts that next time will be too large for even the U.S. government to guarantee.

The question is not whether another crisis of historic proportions will unfold.

The only question is how long we have before that happens, and no one really knows what that time frame might be.

Meanwhile, the interim result has already brought the entire system to the verge of bankruptcy.

One estimate projects a cumulative budget deficit by 2021 of nearly $5 trillion dollars.

But that figure could easily double and approach $10 trillion if more bailouts are required before the system is reformed.

Clearly, embarking on a policy of austerity would be catastrophic.

Continued stimulus is necessary, because the economy will collapse without it.

But continuing to promote debt driven consumption will only prop up the economy until the next financial crisis unfolds and bankrupts the system.

This is why it's imperative to address the underlying problem of slow growth and stagnation that reflects weak demand and has led to the unprecedented accumulation of debt.

While financial regulation is badly needed, speculation and systemic financial risk is simply one manifestation of structural weakness in the productive economy.

When we consider the underlying problem, what becomes clear is the extent of economic leakage in both demand and investment, which wasn't anticipated when supply side policies were put in place in the early 1980s.

Leakage explains why attempts at stimulus have become ineffective.

Stimulus has limited impact, because spending on imports leaks out of the economy.

So while government stimulus is necessary, it largely amounts to propping up demand for cheap imports.

The effect is to perpetuate the global system, by supporting demand for exports from Hong Kong, Taiwan, Malaysia, Singapore, and China.

The only way out of the current predicament is to cultivate growth in ways that avoid this problem of economic leakage.

That means large scale government investment in domestic manufacturing, infrastructure, and advanced technology to offset the long term decline in manufacturing previously discussed.

What will be required, in conjunction with other policies to reduce the trade deficit and reform the financial sector, is a modern form of industrial policy.

It would be a mistake to think of industrial policy as an option we have for the future.

Industrial policy is nothing less than a requirement for the future prosperity of this country.

The economy simply must be restructured in ways that support a transition away from consumptive spending and toward productive investment.

What is equally clear is that we can't rely on the private sector to make that transition on its own.

At the same time, thanks to Wall Street's influence in Washington, de facto industrial policy now in place amounts to wholesale government subsidy and promotion of financial speculation.

Allowing the financial sector to continually jeopardize the economy will, sooner or later, bring a dramatic fall in the value of the dollar.

In the worst case scenario, the dollar could lose its status as reserve currency in the international system.

For the time being that outcome seems unlikely, mainly because of a lack of viable alternatives.

Currently the role of the dollar is being perpetuated by the European debt crisis.

But dollar depreciation along the lines of the 1985-87 devaluation of 50 percent against the Japanese yen and German mark would be immensely destructive.

The U.S. economy is dependent on imports to a far greater extent now than it was in the 1980s.

Demand leakage from spending on imports drives stagnation and low wages at home, which in turn raises demand for cheap imports.

A 50 percent fall in the dollar would raise the price of imports by 100 percent and destroy the economy.

It is imperative to reduce our dependence on imports for the same reason we need to reduce our dependence on foreign debt.

The only reason this country acts as the servant of financial markets is because our dependence on foreign money makes us vulnerable to the whims of foreign investors.

Food for Thought

The financial crisis of 2008 marked the death of the New Economy, in which economic growth is based on debt driven consumption.

Yet policymakers even now appear to be in the early stages of grief, because they are clearly in denial.

Nothing has been done to address the failed model of growth that lead to the current recession.

Having reached the zero bound on interest rates, the Federal Reserve no longer has the option of lowering rates to stimulate demand.

While employment can't improve without domestic investment, private sector investment is $300 - $400 billion a year less than what is needed for recovery.

For the Federal Reserve, the idea of stimulus is to continue buying toxic mortgages from banks to support higher prices in the real estate market.

This is nothing more than a policy of *status quo ante*, in which every effort is made to re-inflate the housing bubble that collapsed in 2008.

Re-inflating the bubble is a recipe for economic collapse, that even by comparison with the Great Depression of the 1930s, could very well be unprecedented.

The stock market and the number of people on food stamps are both at record high levels.

In December 2014 the House of Representatives passed a budget bill that reverses a key provision of the Dodd Frank Act passed in 2010.

The House bill, as well as the Senate version passed in March 2015, allows banks to include derivatives as a class of assets that are covered by federal deposit insurance.

What this means is that when, not if, but when the next financial crisis requires the federal government to bail out the banks, the size of the losses involved will bankrupt the Treasury.

When that happens the dollar will lose its status as the international reserve currency, dollar devaluation will follow, and prices on imports will rise exponentially.

Making productive investments would be a far better use of federal resources than trying to guarantee the unfunded liabilities of Wall Street banks.

Summary

In the late 1970s, high interest rates used to curb inflation caused the dollar to become overvalued, raising the cost of American exports and creating record unemployment.

As a result, manufacturing employment declined by more than 2 million jobs between 1979 and 1982.

The dollar was subsequently devalued, which made imports more expensive and kept the trade deficit in balance through the early 1990s.

In the mid-1990s, currency devaluations in Asia and Latin America returned the dollar to a highly overvalued position.
.
The impact was to make imports far cheaper and drive the trade deficit to unprecedented levels, which also exacerbated the trend toward offshoring.

Between 1998 and 2010 manufacturing employment declined by 6 million jobs.

This loss of manufacturing jobs also brought additional loss of more than 10 million supply chain jobs, and ripple effects that lead to loss of another 7 million jobs throughout the economy.

While 23 million jobs were lost between 1998 and 2010, foreign profits of U.S. corporations have risen from 5 percent in the 1960s to an average 22 percent since 2008.

This country's manufacturing base has been sent overseas, and the employment associated with that production has been lost.

The process has undermined demand, bringing a loss of investment in the U.S. economy.

Compared to the historic average investment of 4 percent GDP, domestic investment has declined dramatically, and since 2005 has averaged just 2.1 percent of GDP.

Between the mid-1980s and 2013, the cumulative value of this investment gap was over $4 trillion dollars.

In the same period, U.S. foreign investment was $4.9 trillion dollars, so that loss of domestic investment has been closely matched by investment overseas.

The loss of more than 23 million jobs between 1998 and 2010 has not been offset by service sector employment.

This fact lays bare the myth that the U.S. is in the process of a natural transition to a Service Economy, in which manufacturing becomes less important in creating value added in the national economy.

Manufacturing provides far greater value added based on economies of scale than other sectors, as well as extensive employment through supply chains that has no comparison in the service sector.

The impact of extensive forward and backward linkages is that when manufacturing declines, the overall economy declines along with it.

As manufacturing goes, so goes the economy.

Offshoring also poses even greater threat to jobs in the service sector than in manufacturing.

Between 30 million and 40 million jobs are vulnerable to offshoring, of which some 90 percent are in services.

Today the trade deficit reflects a leakage of both demand and investment.

Offshoring allocates investment to developing countries, matched by a corresponding decline of investment in the U.S. economy.

Low wage imports have brought stagnant wages and undermined the demand generating process in the domestic economy.

At the same time, asset price inflation based on debt has obscured the fundamental damage to demand in the underlying economy.

Continued reliance on cheap imports and debt driven growth will only prop up the economy until the next financial crisis unfolds and bankrupts the system.

This is why it's imperative to address the underlying problem of slow growth and stagnation that reflects weak demand in the economy.

Leakage explains why attempts at stimulus have become ineffective.

Stimulus has limited impact, because spending on imports leaks out of the economy.

Cultivating growth in ways that avoid this problem of economic leakage will require a modern form of industrial policy.

As an interim measure, continued stimulus is necessary, because the economy will collapse without it.

But the challenge is to restructure the economy in ways that support a transition away from consumptive spending and toward productive investment.

Recreating a viable economy that can generate wealth requires building productive capacity in high value added manufacturing industries.

Government should implement whatever measures necessary to make productive investment more attractive than financial speculation.

Until that objective is achieved, the U.S. economy will be vulnerable to financial collapse that could be far worse than the 2008 crisis.

Conclusion: Mandate for Reform

Since the 1980s, the decline of manufacturing and the rise of finance have created an economy that can't generate enough jobs.

With consumers in debt and incomes stagnant, we spend over $1 trillion dollars a year on imports from low wage countries.

Spending on imports drives growth offshore, instead of driving growth in the U.S. economy.

Three decades of stagnant wages spent on low wage imports have reduced *demand for domestic goods* to a point that it no longer justifies private sector investment.

This is the fundamental problem of the economy today.

Meanwhile the Obama administration and the Federal Reserve remain committed to ongoing stimulus for consumption, augmented by propping up real estate values in the housing market.

Political power is in the hands of those who ignore the danger posed by
- deflation in the real economy, and
- another financial collapse on Wall Street.

This reality of our politics is seen in the bipartisan 2015 budget agreement that includes federal deposit insurance for financial derivatives.

A companion volume, published in conjunction with this book, is *SWIFT Act: Swift Action for Permanent Recovery*.

SWIFT Act outlines five key areas of reform as follows.
- Smart Growth
- Wage Standards
- Industrial Policy
- Financial Reform
- Trade and Tax Reform

The name SWIFT Act also embodies a symbolic message.

SWIFT is an acronym for the Society for Worldwide Interbank Financial Telecommunication.

SWIFT handles financial messaging between member banks and financial institutions engaged in international transactions.

Among these is the Bank of International Settlements, an international organization owned by central bank members in sixty countries.

SWIFT Act proposals send a message to Wall Street and financial interests around the world.

The message is that SWIFT Act marks the beginning of the end of the tyranny of global finance.

Globalism has been revealed as an ideology of financiers, who profit from the destruction of national economies through offshoring.

The *Wall Street/Trade complex* profits from offshoring, and openly sides with China in driving the deindustrialization of America.

Like the battles at Lexington and Concord in 1776, I believe SWIFT Act will come to be known as the shot heard round the world.

SWIFT Act proposals are a road map to long term economic recovery.

Passing those proposals into law will require an epic battle with banks and financial interests that control our government through money in politics.

We need 10 to 20 million signatures on the SWIFT Act petition.

Please visit our website at swiftact.com, and consider adding your endorsement online.

SWIFT Act - Preview

SWIFT Act proposals are revenue neutral, and are based on 5 core principles.

Smart Growth

Permanent recovery can only be achieved through revival of the real economy, led by manufacturing and high technology, high-value-added industries.

Recovery will also require reducing the trade deficit and reforming the financial sector to fundamentally restructure the national economy.

The economy's capacity to create wealth and jobs has declined, because investments that should have been made in productive industry have been used instead for speculative finance or foreign investment.

The country now faces multiple deficits (the federal budget deficit, public investment deficit, private investment deficit, and the trade deficit), which any plan for recovery has to address.

Without slow and distorted growth, there would be no budget deficit.

The goal of Smart Growth reflects acknowledgement that permanent recovery will require economic restructuring.

Wage Standards

Imposing wage standards on imports will prohibit unfair wage competition and reduce offshoring.

American industry can't compete with cheap imports, often made with wages between 50 cents and $1 an hour, and even lower in the use of child labor.

Even so, higher wages in the export sectors of poor countries would have limited impact on prices in the American market.

Corporations can't raise prices without losing sales, because consumers no longer have the income or even the credit to pay higher prices.

Instead, higher wages overseas would raise global demand for U.S. exports.

Increasing U.S. exports would reduce unemployment and spur growth in this country.

The result would be higher demand, in both the U.S. and abroad, which would increase sales and drive economic growth around the world.

Industrial Policy
Strategic promotion of manufacturing and advanced technology industry is critical to U.S. competitiveness in world markets.

Consider that between 1995 and 2010, the U.S. traded places with China in a wide range of manufacturing industries.

In 1995, the U.S. out-produced China 7 to 1 in low, medium, and high technology industries.

But in 2010, China out-produced the U.S. in every category, and by nearly 2 to 1 in medium technology industries.

American industry can't compete with producers that have the support of foreign governments.

Large scale investments in high technology industry are essential to
- support the demand generating process, and
- re-establish the virtuous circle of growth.

What is needed is beyond argument.

But there isn't enough demand in the economy to justify private sector investment.

Without publicly funded investments, the U.S. economy will continue to unravel.
.

Financial Reform
Unprecedented growth of the financial sector has reduced incentive for productive investment and diminished the economy's capacity to create jobs.

At the same time, Wall Street interests and too-big-to-fail banks have successfully lobbied to block meaningful reform.

SWIFT Act proposals address five essential areas of financial reform:

First, reduce systemic risk, by
- requiring separation between commercial banks and investment firms, and
- imposing size limitations to break up the banks and prevent future bailouts, and
- setting limits on the use of leverage throughout the system

Regulatory exemptions for trading in derivatives and foreign currency should also be repealed.

Second, the financial sector should be subject to taxes designed to establish parity between returns from financial investment and the investments needed in productive industry.

There is no chance of restoring productive investment in American industry, without addressing the excess profits generated by financial investment.

Substantial revenue can be generated by a tax of 0.05 percent (one half of one percent) on financial transactions.

That revenue could be used to fund investments in advanced technology industry.

Third, compensating corporate executives with stock options should be outlawed.

No development has done more harm to American industry than the practice of granting stock options to CEOs and other executives.

Defining corporate value in terms of short term stock prices has only served to give Wall Street financial interests leverage over productive lines of business.

CEOs have been paid to downsize operations through layoffs, and to offshore production to low wage countries.

The goal in either case is to maximize profits, and thereby maximize the short term value of company stock.

CEOs have earned hundreds of millions of dollars through stock options, while American industry has been dismantled and sent offshore.

Fourth, the Consumer Financial Protection Bureau should establish a voluntary pension plan for private sector employees.

Today the only option available to some 70 percent of employees is the 401(k), which provides far less benefit for the same contribution as a pension plan.

While 401(k) plans generate $3 billion a year in fees for Wall Street, low retirement income creates a drag on the economy overall.

The fifth area of financial reform is repeal of the Citizens United ruling that allows unlimited contributions to political campaigns.

Politicians of both parties represent the interests of Wall Street banks and U.S. multinationals with offshore production.

Such has been the corrupting influence of money in politics.

It is sheer nonsense to allow unlimited contributions, which are used to perpetuate Wall Street influence in politics.

Trade and Tax Reform
Unrestricted trade has undermined the U.S. economy and diminished the productive capacity of American industry.

A U.S. VAT would tax imports but not exports in the same way the VAT is used in over 150 countries around the world.

A VAT would make exports more profitable and imports less profitable.

The effect would be to create incentive for investment in manufacturing, and disincentive for offshoring.

Notes

Globalism and Decline

Twin Deficits: Financing Decline
James K. Jackson, 2010. *Financing the U.S. Trade Deficit*. (Washington, D.C.: Congressional Research Service).

Francis E. Warnock, 2010. "How Dangerous Is U.S. Government Debt?: The Risks of a Sudden Spike in U.S. Interest Rates." *Capital Flows Quarterly*, Q2. (New York: Council on Foreign Relations).

Menzie D. Chinn, 2005. "Getting Serious About the Twin Deficits." *Council Special Report* No. 10, September. (New York: Council on Foreign Relations).

Globalism and Globalization
Manfred B. Steger, 2009. *Globalisms: The Great Ideological Struggle of the Twenty-First Century* (Third Edition). (New York: Rowman and Littlefield Publishers); John Raulston Saul, 2005, *The Collapse of Globalism and the Reinvention of the World*. (New York: Overlook Press); Clyde Prestowitz, 2010. *Three Billion New Capitalists: The Great Shift of Wealth and Power to the East*. (New York: Basic Books); Clyde Prestowitz, 1989. *Trading Places: How America Allowed Japan to Take the Lead*. (Rutland: Charles E. Tuttle).

Erik S. Reinert, 2008. *How Rich Countries Got Rich: Why Poor Countries Stay Poor*. (New York: PublicAffairs).

Free Trade Origins
Ha Joon Chang, 2008. *Bad Samaritans: The Myth of Free Trade and the Secret History of Capitalism*. (New York: Bloomsbury Press): 40-48.

Clyde Prestowitz, 2010: *The Betrayal of American Prosperity: Free Market Delusions, America's Decline, and How We Must Compete in the Post-Dollar Era*. (New York: Free Press): 45-50.

The American System
Chang, 2008, *Bad Samaritans*: 48-55; Prestowitz, 2010. *The Betrayal of American Prosperity*: 51-56, and 67-72; Patrick J. Buchanan, 2005. *Where the Right Went Wrong: How Neoconservatives Subverted the Reagan Revolution and Hijacked the Bush Presidency*. (New York: St. Martin's Press): 152-158. The definitive source is Michael Hudson, 2010. *America's Protectionist Takeoff: 1815-1914; The Neglected American School of Political Economy*. (Glashütte, Germany: ISLET-Verdag).

Trade and International Security:
Prestowitz, 2010. *The Betrayal of American Prosperity*: 76:88. My discussion of Smoot-Hawley draws on Ibid: 82-84.

Trade and Development:
Chang, 2008, *Bad Samaritans*: 69-74;

96

Network Production and National Policy: Jason Dedrick, 2007. *Who Profits from Innovation in Global Value Chains?* (Syracuse, NY: Syracuse University).

Offshoring is Not Trade: Paul Craig Roberts, 2010. *How the Economy Was Lost.* (Oakland, CA: Counterpunch and AK Press): 74-77.

The Wall Street / Trade Complex

Jagdish Bhagwati, 1998. "The Capital Myth: The Difference between Trade in Widgets and Dollars," *Foreign Affairs*, Volume 77, No. 3, May/June 1998: 7-12.; Robert Wade and Frank Veneroso, 1998. "The Asian Crisis: The High Debt Model Vs. The Wall Street-Treasury-IMF Complex," *New Left Review*, March-April: 3-23.

The Rise of Global Finance
Growth of financial sector and world credit markets: Jeffrey A. Frieden, 2006. *Global Capitalism: Its Fall and Rise in the Twentieth Century.* (New York: W.W. Norton): 380-81. Johnson and Kwak, *13 Bankers:* 59-60;

World Bank loans based on inflated projections: John Perkins, 2004. *Confessions of an Economic Hit Man.* (San Francisco: Berrett-Koehler).

Economic Restructuring:
Richard Peet, 2009. *Unholy Trinity: The IMF, World Bank, and WTO.* Second Edition. (London: Zed Books); Joseph Stiglitz, 2003. *Globalization and Its Discontents.* (New York: W.W. Norton & Company): Chapter 3, 53-88.

Impact of Restructuring: Stiglitz, *Globalization*: 36. Stiglitz concludes IMF policies result in slow growth, which officials try to justify as being short term.

James R. Vreeland, 2003. *The IMF and Economic Development.* (Cambridge: Cambridge University Press): 126. Vreeland's work is a book length study that supports Stiglitz' conclusion: IMF policies result in slow growth, while their justification is ideological and have proven not to be true.

Global Business and U.S. Foreign Policy:
See Stiglitz, *Globalization*: 104, for his diagnosis of the cause of financial crisis in Latin America in the 1980s, versus Asia in the 1990s.

International Institutions and Globalist Ideology:
Stiglitz, 2003, *Globalization*: 19-20.

Bailing Out Creditors
Robin Hahnel, 1999. *Panic Rules: Everything You Need to Know About the Global Economy.* (Cambridge: South End Press).

Anti-inflation Policy and Slow Growth
Stiglitz, 2003, *Globalization*: 149-152.

High Dollar Policy
Richard Duncan, 2009. *The Corruption of Capitalism: A Strategy to Rebalance the Global Economy and Restore Sustainable Growth.* (Hong Kong: CLSA Books): 95-104.

Global Finance and the IMF Agenda:
Stiglitz, 2003, *Globalization*: 45

World Financial Markets
Richard C. Longworth, 1998. *Global Squeeze: The Coming Crisis for First-World Nations.* (Chicago, IL: Contemporary Books): 44-49.

New Role of Finance
Noreena Hertz, 2004. *The Debt Threat: How Debt is Destroying the Developing World and Threatening Us All.* (New York: Harper Collins). Phenomena of Crowding In: Duncan, *Corruption of Capitalism*: 118-123.

Market Globalism: Revolving door between Wall Street and Washington: Simon Johnson and James Kwak, 2010. *13 Bankers: The Wall Street Takeover and the Next Financial Meltdown.* (New York: Vintage Books): *92-100;* Charles Ferguson, 2012. *Predator Nation: Corporate Criminals, Political Corruption, and the Hijacking of America.* (New York: Crown Business): 300-308.

Wall Street-Trade Complex:
Globalization of production creates triple hemorrhage: Thomas Palley, 2012. *From Financial Crisis to Stagnation: The Destruction of Shared Prosperity and the Role of Economics.* (New York: Cambridge University Press): 44-45.

Losing the Trade War
James Mann. 2007. *The China Study: How Our Leaders Explain Away Chinese Repression.* (New York: Viking Penguin).

Peter Navarro. 2011. *Death by China: Confronting the Dragon – A Global Call To Action.* (Upper Saddle River: Prentiss Hall).

Transfer of Technology:
Prestowitz, *Betrayal of American Prosperity*: 207-217; Gary Pisano and Wily C. Shih, 2009. "Restoring American Competitiveness," in *Harvard Business Review* 87, Nos. 7-8 (July-August).

Child Labor
International Programme on the Elimination of Child Labour, 2010. *Global Child Labour Developments: Measuring Trends 2004 to 2008.* (Geneva, Switzerland: International Labour Organization).

Summary
John R. MacArthur, 2012. *The Outrageous Barriers to Democracy in America: Or, Why a Progressive Presidency is Impossible.* (Brooklyn: Melville House). The interview cited was with Bill Moyers.

End Game

Deindustrialization
Josh Bivens, 2003. *Updated Employment Multipliers for the U.S. Economy.* (Washington, D.C.: Economic Policy Institute). No. 268, Table 8.

Robert D. Atkinson, Luke A. Stewart, Scott M. Andes, and Stephen J. Ezell, 2012. "Worse than the Great Depression: What Experts are Missing About American Manufacturing Decline." (Washington, D.C.: Information Technology & Innovation Foundation).

Susan Houseman, 2011. "Offshoring Bias in U.S. Manufacturing" *Journal of Economic Perspectives*, Volume 25, Number 2: 111-132.

For refutation of argument that public investment causes "crowding out" see Robert Pollin and Dean Baker, 2009. "Public Investment, Industrial Policy, and U.S. Economic Renewal," (Amherst, MA: Political Economy Research Institute and Center for Economic and Policy Research), Working Paper Series Number 211: 13.

Michael Mandel and Diana G. Carew, 2012. *Measuring the Real Impact of Imports on Jobs*. (Washington, D.C.: Progressive Policy Institute).

Ron French. 2006. *Driven Abroad: The Outsourcing of America*. (Muskegon: RDR Books).

Ronald Hira and and Anil Hira. 2008. *Outsourcing America: The True Cost of Shipping Jobs Overseas and What Can Be Done About It*. (New York: American Management Association).

Pat Choate, 2008, *Dangerous Business: The Risks of Globalization for America*. (New York: Alfred A. Knopf).

Sherrod Brown, 2006. *Myths of Free Trade: Why American Trade Policy Has Failed*. (New York: W.W. Norton).

Christina D. Romer, 2012. "Do Manufacturers Need Special Treatment?" www.nytimes.com/2012/02/05/business/do-manufacturers-need-special-treatment-economic-view.html Last accessed October 25, 2012.

The Myth of the Service Economy
Alan Blinder, 2009."On the Measurability of Offshorability," http:voxeu.org/article/twenty-five-percent-us-jobs-are-offshorable Last accessed October 24, 2012.

Stephen S. Cohen and John Zysman, 1987. *Manufacturing Matters: The Myth of the Post-Industrial Economy*. (New York: Basic Books).

Susan Helper, Timothy Krueger, and Howard Wial, 2012. *Why Does Manufacturing Matter? Which Manufacturing Matters? A Policy Framework*. (Washington, D.C.: Brookings Institution).

C. Alan Garner, 2004. *Offshoring in the Service Sector: Economic Impact and Policy Issues*. (Kansas City, MO: Federal Reserve Bank of Kansas City). Economic Review, Third Quarter 2004.

The Lender of Last Resort

Duncan, *Corruption of Capitalism*: 95-104.

John Mauldin and Jonathan Tepper, 2011. *Endgame: The End of the Debt Supercycle and How It Changes Everything*. (Hoboken, New Jersey: John Wiley & Sons).

Figure A-1
U.S. Balance of Payments, 2007 (Billions)

	Receipts	Payments	Balance
Current Account			
Merchandise exports	1,163		1,163
Merchandise imports		(1,982)	(1,982)
		Trade balance:	(819)
Net investment income	82		82
Net services	119		119
Net transfers		(113)	(113)
1		Current account balance:	(731)
Capital Account			
Capital outflows		(1,290)	(1,290)
Capital inflows	1,583		1,583
Statistical discrepancy		(43)	(43)
2		Capital account balance:	250
3		Reserve transactions balance: (1) + (2):	(481)
Method of Financing			
4 Increase in domestic reserve assets	0		
5 Decrease in foreign reserve assets	481		
6 Total financing of deficit: (4) + (5)	481		
	Balance of Payments (3) + (6):		0

Source: Format from Frederic S. Mishkin (2012) and Stanley E. Eakins, Financial Markets and Institutions. (Boston: Pearson Education): Chapter 16: Appendix: W-36. Figures from Bureau of Economic Analysis

APPENDIX

The Balance of Payments:
Refer to Table A-1

Receipts column
All money coming into the country is entered in the Receipts column.

Payments column
All money leaving the country is entered in the Payments column.

Current Account
The current account is used to record transactions involving goods and services.

The trade in goods is the difference between merchandise exports and merchandise imports, called the trade balance. In 2007 the U.S. had a trade deficit of $819 billion dollars. The next three items are:

a) Net investment income: the balance of income received from abroad (positive) and foreign income earned on U.S. investments (negative).

b) Net services: the balance of amounts paid for foreign services (negative) and foreign payments coming into the country (positive) for U.S. services.

c) Net transfers: the balance of gifts, pensions, and foreign aid. In 2007 the balance for transfers was $113 billion in money leaving the country, which is entered as a (negative) in the Payments column.

The current account is one side of the ledger, often called the trade side, in the double entry bookkeeping system used for international transactions.

Capital Account
The capital account is used to record transactions involving capital flows between the U.S. and other countries.

a) Capital outflows reflect U.S. purchases of foreign assets. These purchases involve money leaving the country and are entered as a (negative) in the Payments column.

b) Capital inflows reflect foreign purchases of U.S. assets. These purchases create flows of money coming into the country, and are entered as a (positive) in the Receipts column.

c) Statistical discrepancies reflect unrecorded transactions. Because most analysts think the statistical discrepancy reflects hidden capital flows, this item is included in the capital account.

The capital account is the other side of the ledger, often called the financial side, in the double entry bookkeeping system used for international transactions.

Figure A-2
China Balance of Payments, 2007 (Billions of US Dollars)

	Receipts	Payments	Balance
Current Account			
Merchandise exports	1,220		1,220
Merchandise imports		(904)	(904)
		Trade balance:	316
Net investment income	26		26
Net services		(8)	(8)
Net transfers	39		39
1		**Current account balance:**	**373**
Capital Account			
Capital outflows		(848)	(848)
Capital inflows	921		921
Statistical discrepancy	16		16
2		**Capital account balance:**	**89**
3		**Reserve transactions balance: (1) + (2):**	**462**
Method of Financing			
$ Purchase **4** Increase in domestic reserve assets		(462)	
5 Decrease in foreign reserve assets		0	
6 Total offset for surplus: (4) + (5)		**(462)**	
		Balance of Payments (3) + (6):	**0**

Source: Format from Frederic S. Mishkin (2012) and Stanley E. Eakins, Financial Markets and Institutions. (Boston: Pearson Education): Chapter 16: Appendix: W-36. Figures from http://www.safe.gov.cn/ci. Accessed July 2, 2012.

Reserve Transactions Balance

The reserve transactions balance is the sum of the balances on the current account and the capital account:

Current account balance + capital account balance = reserve transactions balance

The reserve transactions balance is the total reserve amount that has to move between central banks to finance international transactions.

This key figure shown on Line 3 is the total account surplus or deficit of any given country in relation to the rest of the world.

In 2007 the U.S. had a reserve transactions deficit of $481 billion dollars.

This reserve deficit has to be offset with another entry, because account balancing is the method of reconciling transactions between the U.S. and the rest of the world.

Balance of Payment accounts are balanced by financing deficits or investing surpluses. The process is referred to as financing the balance of payments.

Financing the Balance of Payments

Line 4 is used to record increases in reserve assets. For example, if the U.S. had increased its holdings of foreign currency in 2007, a (positive) entry would have been made on line 4 for that item.

Line 5 is used to record decreases in foreign reserve assets. Foreign reserve assets decrease when foreign central banks increase their holdings of U.S. dollars and dollar denominated assets.

In 2007 foreign central banks increased their holdings of dollar assets by $481 billion dollars, shown as a (positive) entry for that item.

This entry records an increase in U.S. debt, but is shown as a (positive), because it reflects money coming into the country from foreign banks.

The reserve transactions deficit of $481 billion (negative), plus the financing of $481 billion (positive) received from foreign banks, equals zero.

The balance of payments is therefore zero, meaning the accounts are in balance.

Foreign Countries with Trade Surplus

While the balance of payments system works the same for every country, there are important differences in how the reserve transactions balance is financed.

Most important, foreign countries with a reserve surplus have no choice but to buy dollar assets to offset that surplus.

Table A-2 shows the 2007 balance of payments accounts for China.

Line 3 shows a surplus in reserves equivalent to $462 billion U.S. dollars.

Figure A-3
2007 Reserve Balance Summary for U.S. and China

Financing Reserve Balances - 2007	(Billions of U.S. Dollars)	
	U.S. Receipts	China Payments
Method of Financing		
4 Increase in domestic reserve assets	0	(462) **$ Purchase**
5 Decrease in foreign reserve assets	481	0
6 Total financing of balance: (4) + (5)	**481**	**(462)**

Source: Figures A-1 and A-2.

Line 5 is used to record a decrease in *foreign* reserves, as in the previous discussion of the U.S. balance of payments.

But line 5 in the balance of payments for China, and for other foreign surplus countries, will almost always reflect a very small number or a zero entry.

This occurs because oil and most commodities are denominated in dollars, not in the Chinese yuan, or any other foreign currency.

As a result, a large portion of China's reserve surplus reflects dollar asset transactions. This means in 2007 China had a large surplus of dollar reserves.

Foreign countries offset trade surpluses through the purchase of dollar denominated assets.

Line 4 is used to record increases in domestic reserves. In the balance of payments for China, and for other foreign surplus countries, the increase in domestic reserves is entered as a (negative).

The entry for line 4 is (negative) because it records the purchase of U.S. and other foreign assets, reflecting money flowing out of the country.

As a result, the balance of payments for foreign surplus countries shows a method of financing that is the mirror image of that shown for the U.S.

Table A-3 shows this mirror image in summary form.

This is because the purchase of dollar assets, including U.S. debt instruments, is required to balance the international accounts of foreign surplus countries.

Reader Notes

Reader Notes

Reader Notes

About the Author

I taught political science for five years and received my doctorate from Tulane in 1992. After 20 years in the private sector, my reaction to the Occupy Wall Street movement was to write a series of books and establish the non-profit SWIFT Act Alliance.

The U.S. economy is in crisis, and unprecedented numbers of voters are rejecting the status quo. I wrote these books in the hope of providing a common sense guide to understanding how economies work and why ours no longer functions the way it should.

My goal is to empower readers through explanations that build economic literacy and provide clear discussion of fundamentals that led to the Great Depression and continue today in the Great Recession.

Millions of people realize we can no longer trust the establishment to manage the economy. That means the public will need greater understanding of economic fundamentals to support demands for meaningful reform.

Toward that end, SWIFT Act proposals are intended as a blueprint for what I consider to be essential aspects of reform we need for long term recovery.

Made in the USA
Charleston, SC
17 August 2016